PRIESTHOOD

THE HARD
QUESTIONS

PRIESTHOOD

THE HARD QUESTIONS

Edited by
Gerald P. Gleeson

E.J. DWYER

Priesthood: The Hard Questions is the twentieth book in the FAITH AND CULTURE series. Numbers 1–19 were published by the Catholic Institute of Sydney, St Patrick's College, Manly, NSW, Australia. Numbers 20 and following will be published by E.J. Dwyer (Australia) Pty. Ltd. in association with the Catholic Institute of Sydney.

First published in 1993 by
E.J. Dwyer (Australia) Pty Ltd
3/32-72 Alice Street
Newtown NSW 2042
Australia
Phone: (02) 550 2355
Fax: (02) 519 3218
In association with the Catholic Institute of Sydney

National Library of Australia
Cataloguing-in-Publication data
Priesthood: the hard questions.

ISBN 0 85574 245 3.

1. Priesthood. I. Gleeson, Gerald P. (Gerald Patrick), 1952- .
(Series: Faith and culture).

262.1

ISSN 0156-1960

Edited by Jean Cooney
Cover design by Luc Oechslin, Tatum Graphics, Sydney
Text design by Katrina Rendell
Typeset in 11/12 Andover by Post Typesetters
Printed in Australia by Griffin Paperbacks, Adelaide, SA.

Distributed in Canada by:
  Meakin and Associates
  Unit 17
  81 Auriga Drive
  NEPEAN, ONT K2E 7Y5
  Ph: (613) 226 4381
  Fax: (613) 226 1687

Distributed in Ireland and the UK by:
  Columba Book Service
  93 The Rise
  Mount Merrion
  BLACKROCK CO. DUBLIN
  Ph: (01) 283 2954
  Fax: (01) 288 3770

Distributed in the United States by:
  Morehouse Publishing
  871 Ethan Allen Highway
  RIDGEFIELD CT 06877
  Ph: (203) 431 3927
  Fax: (203) 431 3964

CONTENTS

CONTRIBUTORS

The studies in this volume are the work of priests who are, or have been, on the staff of the Catholic Institute of Sydney, Manly, New South Wales.

Neil Brown is professor of moral theology in the Institute, and founding editor of the *Faith and Culture* Series. He is the author of *The Worth of Persons* (1983), *Christians in a Pluralist Society* (1986), and *Spirit of the World: The Moral Basis of Christian Spirituality* (1990).

Brian Byron has taught theology in the Institute, at Banyo Seminary, Brisbane, and at the Catholic Theological Union, Hunters Hill, Sydney. He is parish priest of Gladesville, and Chair of the Sydney Archdiocesan Ecumenical Commission. He is the author of *Loyalty in the Spirituality of St Thomas More* (1972), *A Theology of Eucharistic Sacrifice* (1974), *Sacrifice and Symbol* (1991), and articles in international journals.

Edmund Campion is associate professor of church history in the Catholic Institute and a well-known Sydney writer. His books include *Lord Acton and the First Vatican Council* (1975), *John Henry Newman: Friends, Allies, Bishops, Catholics* (1980), *Rockchoppers* (1982) and *Australian Catholics* (1987).

David Coffey is professor of dogmatic theology in the Catholic Institute of Sydney. Author of many articles in international theological journals, his major works include *Grace: The Gift of the*

Holy Spirit (1979), *Believer, Christian, Catholic* (1986), and a forth-coming study on the Trinity.

Gerald Gleeson teaches philosophy in the Catholic Institute. After reading philosophy at the University of Cambridge he completed his doctorate at the University of Leuven with a dissertation entitled *The Significance of Metaphor*. He is the author of articles in the *Irish Theological Quarterly, Pacifica, Literature and Aesthetics, The Australasian Catholic Record* and the *Faith and Culture* Series.

David Orr is a Benedictine monk at Arcadia, New South Wales. His doctoral studies at the Pontifical Liturgical Institute, Rome, centered on the liturgy of confirmation. He is parish priest of Arcadia, and part-time lecturer in liturgy in the Catholic Insti-tute of Sydney.

After teaching theology in the Catholic Institute for a number of years, **David Walker** became the founding director of the Educational Centre for Christian Adult Education, Rand-wick, New South Wales. He is a widely known lecturer in spirituality and author of numerous articles in religious and educational journals. He is the chairperson of the Australian Consortium of Experiential Education, author of *God is a Sea* (1977) and coeditor of *Reflection: Turning Experience into Learning* and *Experience and Learning: Reflection at Work*.

William Wright is a graduate in history from the University of Sydney. He is engaged in parish ministry at Mt Druitt, in western Sydney, and is part-time lecturer in church history at the Catholic Institute. He is the author of *St Patrick's College: One Hundred Years* (1992), and articles in *Faith and Culture, The Journal of the Australian Catholic Historical Association*, and *The Australasian Catholic Record*.

INTRODUCTION

Priesthood as Metaphor for Ordained Ministry

Gerald P. Gleeson

"The goal of the ordained ministry is to serve this priesthood of all the faithful."[1] These words of the 1973 Anglican-Roman Catholic International Commission report, *Ministry and Ordination*, recapitulate a decisive shift in the Catholic understanding of ordained ministry during the latter half of the twentieth century. No longer is the priest elevated as a more or less isolated mediator *between* God and the Christian people. Rather, the ordained priest finds his identity *within* the community of the church, enabling the church to be and become more truly itself. As John Thornhill has written:

> ...the ordained minister is one who *with his whole existence* is given to serving those things which make the Church to be what God has called it to be in his gracious plan for humanity.[2]

Linguistically, this renewed understanding of priesthood is reflected in the fact that "priest" is no longer the central or dominant theological concept by which ecclesial leadership is characterized. The crucial realities are *ministry* and *ordination*, both understood more broadly than in the recent past: the ordained person is ordained to a threefold ministry of *word*, *sacrament*, and *pastoral care*; and ordination itself takes one of three forms: *bishop*, *presbyter* or *deacon*.

I

Recent developments in the theology of ordained ministry can be clarified by our recognizing the distinction between the *meaning* and the *referent* of the term "priest". In ordinary usage "priest" refers to ordained ministers as the subjects of whatever is said to be applicable to them. Thus one might say, *"priests exercise a threefold ministry of word, sacrament and pastoral care"*, or "priests need also to be prophets", and so on. By contrast, the meaning of the *term* "priest", what is understood and evoked by it, is more narrowly circumscribed (cf. the Latin *sacerdos*). One thinks of official, sacred, mediating, and cultic figures defined chiefly in relation to religious ritual, and the offering of sacrifice in particular.

> In the ancient religions, the priests are the ministers of worship, the guardians of the sacred traditions, the spokesmen of the divinity in their capacity as divines.[3]

While the mediating role of the priests of the First Covenant with Israel involved teaching functions in addition to ritual functions, the latter sacrificial role was paramount.[4] Indeed, it is precisely because of this focal meaning—the relationship with ritual sacrifice—that Christian traditions have disputed the applicability of the term "priest" to the ordained ministers of the New Covenant.

For those churches which have kept the term "priest", it is emblematic of much that they hold true of the church's structure and sacramental economy. Yet even in these churches the development of a more inclusive understanding of ordained ministry has turned on the recognition that the term "priest" cannot by itself embrace all that needs to be said about ordained Christian ministry. As the report of the Australian Lutheran-Roman Catholic Dialogue on the ordained ministry remarks of Catholic teaching, "ordained ministry in the church cannot be envisaged (as has happened in the past) outside of [the] threefold ministry of Christ" as teacher, high priest, and shepherd.[5]

This inclusive theology of ordained ministry is also more faithful to the origins of Christian ministry as they have been revealed by a heightened awareness of its complex history down the centuries, along with an ecumenical willingness to avoid the constricting emphases engendered by past controversies.

Yet, despite these theological advances, pastoral and doctrinal difficulties over ordained ministry still abound. In most of the industrial world, the decline in the number of those offering themselves for ordination in the Catholic church continues with little sign of abating. Obligatory celibacy for diocesan priests is questioned by many, and the reasons for the Catholic church's exclusion of women from ordination are unpersuasive. Indeed, in many parts of the Catholic world the fundamental question as to whether *anyone* should be "set apart", ordained to a lifelong and distinctive ministry of leadership and spiritual "authority", is either being asked explicitly or is implicit in various attempts at more "democratic" and participatory models of leadership.

As a result some Catholics today fear that the renewed emphasis on the ordained minister's position within, and as representative of, the community is leading to a loss of the traditionally "high" theology of the Catholic priest as "representative of Christ" without which, they suppose, "it is difficult to see any particular worth in being a priest at all".[6] Others, like Edward Schillebeeckx, have argued that the church must take a more open approach to the forms and structures of ministry which embody its "human face".[7]

The studies in this book help to situate these continuing debates within the Catholic church, and suggest ways of resolving the pastoral and doctrinal issues they raise. From their different perspectives—historical, liturgical, pastoral and dogmatic—these studies enable us to reconsider the influence which the *metaphor* of priesthood has exercised over the theology of ordained ministry. By locating the realities signified by the concept of priesthood within an inclusive theology of ordained ministry, these studies invite us to a more balanced understanding of Christian priesthood in its twofold expression—as priesthood of all believers and as ministerial priesthood—thereby avoiding the extremes of either "high" or "low" theology in isolation.

II

Today's theology of ordained ministry derives largely from an acknowledgment of its complex and varying history. Our studies commence with David Walker's review of this historical evolution from the distinctive viewpoint of *spirituality*. We thus approach the history of ordained ministry as lived experience, as a form of Christian vocation, and by attention to the models and metaphors by which it has been understood. As Walker shows, the metaphors of "leader", "priest", "cleric", and "monk" have each influenced the theology and practise of ministry in decisive ways.

Early in the history of the Christian movement, the minister was the community *leader* who, above all, was expected to model discipleship for its members. Sharing a similar style of life and employment to other members of the "household of the faith", leaders built up the community by exemplifying the ideals of discipleship to which all were called. This perspective has once again been brought to the fore by the Second Vatican Council's declaration that *all* Christian men and women are called to holiness.[8]

However, for most of the church's history the discipleship model of ministry has been overshadowed by models, especially those of *priest* and *cleric*, which tend to separate the ordained and the non-ordained. Ordination to mission has been reduced to ordination to a distinct state of life. Recognition of the power these models have exercised leads Walker to ask whether the spirituality of the ordained should be defined in terms of their *ministry* or in terms of their discipleship as *ministers*.

The former path is that usually taken in presentations of priestly spirituality; priests are encouraged "to become what they are", that is, to form their lives, their personalities and spiritualities in terms of one or other objectified model of ministry proposed to them. It is obvious how the seminary formation of young, immature Christian men has been directed towards their appropriating a separate and distinctive style of life and spirituality deemed characteristic of priests.

Without deprecating the value of this approach, Walker notes the dangers of endorsing it uncritically. Models of ministry soon become dated. Ministers formed by a dated model of ministry become alienated from their own experience of discipleship, and lose touch with their communities. Walker encourages us to rediscover the alternative approach which would understand ministry in terms of the "personal holiness of the minister" as disciple, thereby highlighting the gifts and uniqueness of individuals, called to shape their ministry around their distinctive path of discipleship. From this viewpoint, the basis for Christian ordination is mature, not immature, discipleship.

Clerical separation is the theme of Edmund Campion's study of medieval priestly life. Campion traces the liturgical and thence juridical separation of the "chosen" (*cleros*), a separation evident above all in the obligatory celibacy of Roman Catholic priests. Studying little known English ecclesiastical sources, Campion shows how celibacy was gradually (and successfully) imposed on the clergy, and how this practice was reinforced by a new theology of the eucharist, epitomized by the eleventh century "liturgical modernism of the silent Canon men", whose inaudible prayer separated their actions from those of the community who became observers of eucharistic worship rather than celebrants in their own right.

Campion shows how eucharistic theology and obligatory celibacy were linked. The corporeality of the eucharistic body of Christ was said to demand the celibacy of the priest, for just as the Virgin Mary brought Jesus into the world, so the ordained priest must be worthy of bringing the eucharistic Jesus into the world. The priest was no longer primarily the "spokesman of the offering community", but was "the representative of God bestowing Himself as gift".

The thirteenth century saw the culmination of a "high" theology of priesthood and eucharist. By the fifteenth century it was clear that a priesthood shaped by this theology alone could no longer meet the pastoral needs of Christendom. Indeed, as William Wright remarks (chapter 4), while there were more than enough men in holy orders, "of the notion that there should be a particular ministry attached to ordination we see little evidence". What we know as parish ministry was in the hands of poorly-qualified men whose work, income and status was menial.

Wright studies the growing demand in this era for *educated* preachers and *pastoral* ministers—a demand evident prior to the Reformation itself. He endorses John Bossy's thesis that between the fifteenth and seventeenth centuries Western Christianity, in both Protestant and Catholic forms, changed from being a communal religion cemented by the bonds of kinship to being a religion of the Word, and of individual responsibility under God.[9] With respect to the ordained ministry, this transition is reflected in the transition from "clerk-in-orders" to our modern conception of the "clergyman" as pastoral minister, from celebrant of sacred rites to educated teacher of the faith. The Council of Trent established seminaries precisely to educate a new breed of Catholic priest to meet this new need for teachers of "a faith one could hold, rather than simply belong to".

Unlike the Protestant reformers, however, the Catholic reformers maintained in addition to the preaching role those traditional elements of priesthood—of indelible character, of offering sacrifice, of acting *in persona Christi*—which Luther had discarded. Wright notes that the Reformation "did not invent a new model of ministry; its originality lay in abolishing all other forms of priestly life". Yet, while Trent affirmed the sacrificial character of the mass, it quietly responded to the reformers' criticism of the multiplication of masses: "in practice the bottom dropped out of the Purgatory market... The days when the Catholic church could or would maintain an army of priests simply to sing for the dead were passing away." Henceforth, in practice, both Catholic and Protestant ministers exercised a more diverse and more demanding ministry—celebrating the liturgy, preaching and instructing, giving good example in piety and morality, and exercising pastoral care.

Like all good historical inquiry, Wright's account frees us from fixation with the recent past. With the tensions of the Reformation era behind us, Christians of all traditions are now in a better position to develop a theology of ordained ministry that balances those various elements which, taken in isolation, different denominations have in the past highlighted to the detriment of others.

III

These historical studies both invite and require us to question the extent to which the theology of ordained ministry should be governed by a theology of priesthood. Later chapters introduce a systematic response to this question in terms of four key issues: the status of the term "priest" in the New Testament, the priesthood of all the Christian faithful, the nature of priestly representation, and the spiritual authority of the priest in relation to the Christian conscience.

As Brian Byron notes, what is remarkable about the New Testament's use of the term *priest* is not that it is not used of ordained leaders, but that even its application to the Christ is so rare: indeed it occurs only in the *Letter to the Hebrews'* remarkable theology of Jesus as "high priest". Byron argues, in opposition to most writing on priesthood, that Jesus is (only) *metaphorically* a priest. He was not literally a priest (as indeed *Hebrews* 8:4 notes)—that is, not literally a cultic figure who offered ritual sacrifice. The genius of the author of *Hebrews*, however, was to seize upon the systematic metaphor, or model, of priesthood, sacrifice and cult, in order to re-interpret the significance of Jesus' death and resurrection. As Byron emphasizes, to recognize that the language of priesthood in *Hebrews* is metaphorical is in no way to diminish the reality of the Christ event; it is simply to clarify the way in which this language is being used, and thereby to resolve some long-standing puzzles about how the eucharistic sacrifice itself should be understood.

A surprising corollary of Byron's approach, however, is that the ordained minister is *literally* a priest (*sacerdos*); that is, he is, among other things, a cultic figure, who enacts a ritual sacrifice with the eucharistic elements and thereby continues the church's interpretation of the Christ event as priestly sacrifice. By contrast, the priesthood of all Christian disciples is metaphorical: their lives and praise of God are not literally cultic, even though it is appropriate to portray them in this way. By distinguishing between literal and metaphorical priesthood Byron is able to explain the Second Vatican Council's declaration of the *difference in kind* between the priesthood of the faithful and the ordained priesthood.

Byron's account contrasts sharply with that of much traditional theology. On the traditional view, the cultic priests of the Old Testament foreshadowed the "true" and exemplary priesthood of Christ, in which later ordained Christian priests "participate". The outlook here is Platonic: Christ's high priesthood is the paradigm against which all other instances of priesthood are measured. Byron's account is more Aristotelian. The meaning of the Christ event is in truth beyond all human categories, but human categories must be used to evoke and signify it. Hence, the paradigms of "priesthood" are those provided by human religious practice, specifically that of Judaism and Christianity. Within these traditions we find figures who are literally priests, who offer cultic sacrifice. Christian priests are those cultic figures who literally enact the cultic symbolization and sacramental realization of the Christ event among us.

To ensure that Byron's argument is not misunderstood, another comparison may be helpful. Jesus was not literally a shepherd, but is described *metaphorically* as "the true shepherd". Christian bishops and priests may also be said (metaphorically) to be shepherds of their people. This apt metaphor both characterizes Jesus' relationship with his disciples and provides a model for ordained ministers to imitate. But whereas Jesus was only metaphorically a priest, and ordained ministers only metaphorically shepherds, ordained ministers are *literally* priests, truly cultic figures, whose "mediating" role receives crucial cultic expression in the sacramental economy of the church's life. This fact may help to explain just why priesthood has been taken to be the predominant feature of ordained ministry, such that the ordained have come to be known simply as "priests". Furthermore, it may be that the metaphor of priesthood as involving the cultic offering of (bloody) sacrifice—traditionally a male role—has been one of the powerful, if unacknowledged, motives for the exclusion of women from priestly ordination.

But ordained Christian ministers are not only "priests", not simply cultic figures. Byron's argument reinforces the theme of this book by helping to loosen the tie between priesthood and ordained ministry, for "(cultic) priest" is not the "integrating or governing concept of ordained ministry". The Australian Lutheran-Roman Catholic report quoted earlier observes that:

the Roman Catholic Church regards the mediating role of the ordained ministry to be directed particularly toward the Eucharist, and to find its consummation there.[10]

But even if the mediating role of the ordained minister—his action "in the person of Christ" the One Mediator—integrates this threefold ministry of word, sacrament and pastoral leadership, it does not follow that this mediation should be understood in predominantly cultic terms. The precise meaning of action "in the person of Christ" will be a major theme of David Coffey's study. It is enough to note at this point that it remains an open question just how much the metaphor of *cultic mediation* should be allowed to influence our understanding of ordained ministry—arguably not sufficient to warrant the exclusion of women from a *Christian* priesthood for which cultic sacrifice is but one aspect among many.

Indeed, as David Orr's study shows, "priesthood" is a term which belongs in the first instance to all believers. After centuries of neglect during which "priest" has been confined to the ordained, the priesthood of all the faithful is beginning to receive its theological due. In the early centuries Christian initiation included the imposition of hands as a sign of the gift (or spiritual anointing) of the Holy Spirit to empower the twofold "spiritual sacrifice" of Christian existence: as witness in the world and as liturgical self-offering. Orr shows how, due to the developing liturgy of confirmation, the anointing with the Spirit, signified originally by the imposition of hands, came to be confounded with, indeed reduced to, the *physical anointing* with oil after baptism. This physical anointing was held to signify priestly dignity, while the subsequent imposition of hands in confirmation was held to signify the gift of the Spirit to strengthen a Christian to face the trials of life.

What was lost through these developments was the awareness that the *priestly* dignity of every Christian is rooted in the *spiritual anointing* with the gift of the Holy Spirit, of which the imposition of hands is the outward sign. Ignorant of its truly spiritual priestly dignity, "the community lost its ability to exercise its priesthood in the liturgical celebration" and so its "dependence upon an intermediary priesthood became apparent". Orr summarizes recent theological developments which have recovered the insight that, in virtue of their spiritual anointing, all the assembled faithful truly—not just metaphorically—"celebrate" the eucharistic sacrifice; they do not worship the eucharistic Christ from afar.

The occurrence of "not metaphorically" is this last sentence may seem to conflict with Byron's argument that the priesthood of the faithful is metaphorical rather than literal because their Christian witness is not primarily liturgical. But the two accounts are compatible: the eucharist is a ritual celebration of the self-offering of the whole community viewed (that is, metaphorically) as a priestly people. But the celebration is presided over by one who is (literally, though not simply) a cultic figure, an ordained presbyter ministering to a priestly (albeit non-cultic) people whose self-offering is realized in secular living.

IV

The core of Catholic belief in the sacramentality of the priest's liturgical role is the claim that he represents Christ (or acts *"in persona Christi"*). This claim also lies at the heart of many arguments against the ordination of women, and is central to that "high" theology of priesthood which some fear is now under threat. Talk of "high" and "low" theologies will recall similar issues in Christology, and this comparison is explored in David Coffey's study of priestly representation and women's ordination. As in Christology, "descending" and "ascending" theology are complementary and are required jointly for an adequate theological understanding.

Coffey explores this complementarity in terms of the relationship between the two key features of ordained ministry, as action representative of the church and as action representative of Christ (*in persona Ecclesiae* and *in persona Christi*). He shows how the ordained minister "directly" represents the church in its apostolic succession, and thereby "indirectly" (though immediately) represents Christ as head of the church. This indirect representation of Christ, even in the celebration of the eucharist, is evident in the form of the eucharistic prayer, "in which the priest speaks throughout of Christ in the third person, clearly as someone other than himself, even in the pronunciation of the words of consecration".

Priestly representation occurs on three levels: as apostolic succession, as representation of the church, and as representation of Christ. Coffey examines the implications of each of these aspects for the question of women's ordination. Only the third mode of representation suggests obstacles to the ordination of women, once representation of Christ is linked to a further metaphor of Christ as bridegroom of the church his bride. Having outlined a non-discriminatory Christian anthropology, Coffey asks whether, in the celebration of the eucharist, the priest represents Christ precisely as bridegroom of the church? He concludes that, at most, we find in the liturgy an "allusion" to the image of Christ as bridegroom, an allusion which on its own is insufficient to warrant the exclusion of women. The question as to whether there are other grounds for the exclusion of women from ordination as a divine rather than a human tradition remains open.

One of the most crucial and powerful aspects of priestly ministry has concerned the guidance of conscience. The decline in the practice of individual confession of sin, in most Western countries at least, points to a further decisive shift in the practice and theology of ordained ministry. In the concluding chapter Neil Brown explores this issue in relation to the formation of Christian conscience.

The church is a communion of faith which includes a commitment to the values of the gospel, embodied in concrete moral norms governing Christian living. Recognition of the freedom and responsibility of conscience, however, has opened "personal space" for individuals to grow into the truth of gospel living. In the light of our renewed understanding of the ordained minister's place within the community of faith, Brown examines the way in which the ordained minister ought to assist the moral growth of individual Christians. Priests and people must be together engaged in a "mutually enriching" growth in moral wisdom and witness to the gospel. In developing his account of such a ministry, Brown clarifies the nature of Christian conscience and its right formation, and so the place of dissent within the unity of the church.

Together these studies provide historical and systematic perspectives on Christian priesthood in its two forms—as *universal* priesthood of all Christ's faithful and as *ministerial* priesthood of the ordained. Christians form a priestly people summoned to offer a "spiritual"—that is, Spirit-enabled—sacrifice of witness in the world, which they celebrate in liturgy. The priesthood of their ordained leaders differs in kind not degree: *to be ordained* priest (as bishop, presbyter or deacon) is not to become a better or fuller Christian, it is to be designated on the basis of one's baptism to a specified *and therefore limited* role within the Christian community, a role which both shapes and is shaped by one's gifts and personal holiness as disciple. That role is to build up the priestly holiness of all God's people baptized in Christ.

Christ has instituted ordained ministry for shepherding God's people, for public preaching, and for the administration of the sacraments. Since these means of grace are the Spirit's instruments for creating and preserving faith and for bringing people into God's family, the church through all its history is bound to this ministry.[11]

---

[1] *Anglican-Roman Catholic International Commission, Final Report*, CTS/SPCK, London: 1982, 33
[2] John Thornhill, "The Role of the Ordained Minister within the Christian Community", *The Australasian Catholic Record*, LXVII, 1990, 197

[3] Augustin George, "Priesthood", *Dictionary of Biblical Theology*, ed. X. Leon-Dufour, 2nd edn., G. Chapman, London, 1973, 461

[4] Augustin George, op. cit.

[5] *Pastor and Priest*, A Report from the Australian Lutheran-Roman Catholic Dialogue on the Ordained Ministry in the Life of the Church, Adelaide, 1989, s. 45; cf. *Lumen Gentium*, s. 25

[6] Cf. Patrick J. Dunn, *Priesthood: a Re-examination of the Roman Catholic Theology of the Presbyterate*, Alba House, New York, 1990, 160–164

[7] Edward Schillebeeckx, *The Church with a Human Face—A New and Expanded Theology of Ministry*, Crossroad, New York, 1985

[8] Cf. for e.g. Second Vatican Council, *Lumen Gentium*, s. 32(d)

[9] John Bossy, *Christianity in the West: 1400–1700*, Oxford University Press, Oxford, 1985

[10] Australian Lutheran-Roman Catholic Report, s. 46

[11] Ibid., s. 32

ONE

Models of Spirituality for Ordained Ministers

David Walker

INTRODUCTION

In recent times, there has been great interest in the nature of ordained ministry. It has led to several studies of its development over the centuries, and a number of important developmental stages have been recognized. While there is by no means universal agreement on particular issues, the trends that I would like to focus on in this chapter do have a general measure of agreement, though there are certainly disputes about their significance. The clearer understanding of the development of ordained ministry has raised issues about its nature, which is an important contemporary theological issue. This chapter is not meant to enter into the theological debates about ministry, but rather to see how the development has influenced the spirituality associated with ministry.

The spirituality associated with ministry refers basically to the way ministry is understood and lived. It has been influenced by movements within the Christian tradition. These movements have already been recognized and researched, but their implications for spirituality have not been developed. It is not as if each of these movements was begun and completed within a short time. Each represents a strand that has run through the life of the church over a long period of time. Each of these strands has left its mark on the understanding of ordained ministry today, and the way those who exercise it are expected to live their Christian life. It is not to say that any one particular thing has come to ordained ministry from any one movement, even though in particular cases it might have, but to suggest that what is associated with ordained ministry today has been influenced by these various movements.

Spirituality is often rooted in a particular view of the mystery that lies at its heart, and it is from this that a particular lifestyle and individual practices flow. Often a conversion event involves a particular experience of the mystery, which shapes the way of life that the person adopts. The conversion experiences of Paul, the call of Isaiah, illustrate the point. The aspect of the mystery contained in these events, the relationship between the believer and Jesus, and the holiness of God, influenced the life and message of these two prophetic figures. The particular lifestyle and practices which flow from a particular insight into ministry are meant to reinforce and proclaim that insight into ministry. Spirituality of ministry involves not only a particular way of looking at ministry and living it, but also the particular practices and activities which are associated with this way of perceiving ministry, and which reinforce it.

This issue is important because of the essential relationship between spirituality and ministry. I have indicated elsewhere my belief that spirituality must be the foundation of effective ministry.[1] It is important therefore to reflect on how it has been influenced by different understandings of ministry, and on whether spirituality is a characteristic of ministry itself or of the minister, and how these two approaches affect our appreciation of ministry and its practice.

There is an important interaction between ministry and the spirituality associated with it. Ministry, like spirituality, only exists in its embodiment in a particular person, the minister. I believe it is a mistake to think that one can work out the spirituality of ministry purely from the concept of ministry itself. This can lead to a spirituality which is imposed on individuals and particular communities without any reference to the particular character of the person, and the cultural situation within which that person must exercise the ministry. The more recent traditional approach to spirituality of ordained ministry has been to deduce it from the nature of ministry and impose it on the minister.

The spirituality associated with ministry is essential for ministry. Ordained ministry is not something that is disembodied. It exists in a person, the minister, and it exists for persons, the Christian community. It is a central aspect of the church's mission of preaching the gospel, of evangelization. Paul VI asserted that the axis of evangelization was faithfulness to the message we have received and faithfulness to the people to whom we preach it.[2] While it is important, it is not enough to keep intact the tradition from which we come. This has to be done in a way that is relevant to the age in which we live, and the people to whom we preach it. Applying this to ministry, it is important for the minister to have a spirituality that is relevant to the people who are served. If it is not relevant to them and their culture, the very nature of ministry is overshadowed, and a particular irrelevant spirituality comes to give an interpretation of ministry which distorts its true nature and role. This can happen when a spirituality associated with ministry flows over into a different age in which new insights and new expectations of ministry emerge. The effectiveness of ministry is diminished due to its spirituality, that is its lifestyle and practices, being foreign to the present age. While there may be faithfulness to the tradition, there is not faithfulness to the people being served. It can happen that some will fight for a particular way of living ministry, which may well be an aspect of a former spirituality of ministry, rather than a characteristic of ministry itself. It can also happen that in clinging to these elements we then try to theologize them into the nature of ministry itself, and thus preserve them at the expense of a real understanding of ministry.

Like any aspect of the Christian mystery, ministry needs to become enculturated. However this is not a practice that happens once and is valid for every culture. It is an ongoing, evolving process, in which ministry finds expression in many different cultures. To have ministry and its spirituality defined in terms of one culture is as wrong as having the whole Christian message defined in terms of one culture. This process of enculturation is expressed particularly in the spirituality of the ministry.

My reason for embarking on this chapter is that I believe the spirituality associated with ministry today is the accumulation of many spiritualities from the past. Ordained ministry has been influenced by many models, each contributing to how it is understood and lived. However, the various models have often continued to develop, while the effect they have had on ordained ministry remains static. Perhaps the styles adopted in the light of the differing emphases on priesthood may have been valid in their time. However, what remains is a hotch-potch that needs to be re-evaluated in the light of a contemporary understanding of ordained ministry. This chapter looks at how the present spirituality associated with ministry has developed. Central to it is a brief presentation of the historical developments that have shaped the present understanding of ordained ministry and the lifestyle and practices associated with it.

THE NEW TESTAMENT: THE MINISTER AS DISCIPLE OF JESUS

It would be difficult to assert that the ministerial structure that we have now in the church was already in place in the New Testament. Recent studies of ministry in the New Testament indicate how difficult it is to focus on any particular church order present throughout that period. It is the very diversity of ministry that is its principal characteristic.[3] It is difficult to reconcile this diversity with any one church order or organizational system. It was a time of evolution, and the evolution would continue to take place for well over a hundred and fifty years after the death of Jesus. Even then, the forms which evolved continued to evolve: some of them would not endure in a permanent way in the church, and even those that later became definitive did not exist in their later forms in this earliest period. The terms applied to various ministries were also in a state of evolution. Such terms as *episkopos*, *presbyter*, and *deakonos* were used at this earliest stage, but they did not yet fully embody the meanings they would have later.

The concept of ordained ministry belongs to a later age, though obviously what was to emerge was in some way contained in what had gone before. However, there was a variety of ministries in the earliest Christian community, and it would be a mistake to think that any one of them was the particular ministry that later became ordained ministry. Therefore, to explore the spirituality associated with ministry, I will draw on those references to ministry where some reflection is possible in terms of the spirituality associated with it. The focus of our interest is on how exercising a ministry affects the life of the minister.

The real focus of the New Testament teaching was not so much ministry as discipleship; how to be a follower of Jesus. Ministry arose to serve believers in their efforts to be disciples of Jesus or to draw others to discipleship. This placed great importance on those in ministry to manifest the qualities and virtues associated with being a follower of Jesus. Paul began an emphasis on leadership as the embodiment of what discipleship demands. In himself, in his own life, he offered the witness to Christian discipleship, and called on believers to imitate him: "Take me as your model, as I take Christ."[4] Jesus himself is the model of Christian living, and it is his way of life that Paul reflects to believers. He even sends Timothy to the Corinthians to remind them of how he lives in Christ.[5] Discipleship is something that can be modeled, and leadership should be the appropriate model. The teaching on imitation is central to Paul's understanding of his ministry.[6]

The role of the leader as an example to believers is taken up explicitly in some of the later letters of the New Testament.[7] In the way they speak and behave, leaders are to be an example to their flock. They are to embody in themselves the love, faith and purity expected of every believer.[8] Paul is even presented as working for his living in order that he can give appropriate example to the believers at Thessalonica.[9] The overall focus here is on the Christian life itself, and ministry is seen as embodying it, and proclaiming it in word and deed to believers. Indeed, every believer who takes up what is modeled in leadership becomes a model for fellow believers.[10] Ministry is seen as in the service of discipleship, and therefore requires as its most essential characteristic this very discipleship. Witness is an essential aspect of Christian ministry.

Clearly leadership carried with it responsibility; certain attitudes and qualities came to be associated with those who exercised leadership within the community. They were to exercise their role willingly, eagerly and gladly, not just as a duty or for money.[11] They were not to be dictators.[12] They must not consider themselves above the community, as the Gentile leadership did, but rather as the servants of it, in imitation of Jesus who came not to be served but to serve.[13] Ministry is service. This is illustrated in John's account of Jesus washing the feet of the disciples: "If I then, your Lord and Teacher, have washed your feet, you also ought to wash one another's feet."[14] This aspect of leadership is simply an application of the demands of discipleship: don't look to your own advantage, but to that of others;[15] don't yield to self-indulgence but rather live out the gifts of the Spirit;[16] no one is to exaggerate their own importance.[17] The qualities of love that apply to all Christians should apply especially to those in ministry.[18]

In the early New Testament period ministry was not the object of reflection. It was present not so much as a reality in itself, but as a service or function within the community. It was only towards the later period of the New Testament that it came to be the object of reflection. In the *Letter to the Ephesians* we have a view of ministry as "proclamation, leadership and building up the community in accordance with its apostolic foundations".[19] However, in the New Testament, it was not a question of theologizing about church ministry and then deducing a structure from it. The development took place and then the theologizing. The theologizing came after the evolution; the practice preceded the theory.[20] In this later period one does find reflection on the qualities of those who exercise various ministries.[21] However, most of the elements which emerge are still basic characteristics of the 'Christian life itself; while others are linked to the particular function to be performed. No special lifestyle is yet being singled out.

It seems clear from the New Testament evidence that the spirituality of leadership was not very different from the spirituality of discipleship. Most people in ministry probably continued with their normal life, and served the community from that base. This was the foundation of their example and witness, and they were chosen according to this.

As ministries developed and became clearer, it was more evident what particular qualities or skills were needed for them, but the underlying spirituality remained basically that of Christian discipleship. At this stage, ministry itself did not demand a particular lifestyle, other than that of Christian discipleship. A person was commissioned for ministry rather than ordained for life. We also find ministry associated more with leadership of the community than with liturgical leadership.

THE ORDAINED MINISTER AS *EPISKOPOS*

By the end of the second century, the diversity and plurality of New Testament ministries had developed into a fixed church order, centered round the *episkopos*. The issue here is not simply that one ministry has emerged over and above other ministries. It is rather that the previous diversity has come to be subsumed in this one, and even though the ministries of presbyter and deacon continued to exist, they did so in relationship to this ministry of *episkopos*. This development was by no means uniform, and the influences giving rise to it were varied.[22] It was an important development, and was to remain the focus of church structure from this time on. Our aim is to reflect on the significance of this development for an understanding of the spirituality that has been associated with ordained ministry.

Discussing the relationship between *presbyteroi* and *episkopoi* in the period prior to the end of the second century, Tavard proposes "All the evidence suggests that these fulfilled, at first, identical or at least similar offices, to which different names were assigned in different places.... For my part, I hold that history favors a fundamental identity of priesthood and episcopacy, rather than the theory of an intrinsic difference between them".[23] In the New Testament, the difference between these two ministries is not clear. What is clear is that by the end of the second century the *episkopos* had emerged as the figure with authority, the major leader within the Christian community. He began to be seen as specifically different, and the *presbyteroi* were seen in relationship to him. He now becomes the model for ordained ministry, and how the *episkopos* is understood will affect the understanding of ordained ministry: for example it is the *episkopos* to whom the term "priest" is applied by Cyprian, and it then pervades all the understanding of ordained ministry.

We have some insights into the role of the *episkopos* at this time. The "apostolic tradition" of Hippolytus (about 200 AD) presents the ministry of the *episkopos* in terms of pastoral leadership and exemplarity of Christian life. The liturgical role of the *episkopos* is not the primary focus. Ministry did not emerge in relationship to the eucharist. It came out of the need to build community: preaching, admonition, leadership were the key elements in ordained ministry as it was embodied in the *episkopos*.[24] At this time there was no special emphasis on the relationship between ministry and eucharist as central to the role of the ordained ministry, even though there was clearly a liturgical role.

Origen offers another insight from this time. For him the proper vocation of the *episkopos* is to be a religious example and sympathetic physician of the soul to his congregation. He laments that they have become worldly-minded, caught up in earthly occupations, seekers of wealth and land, the subjects of flattery and corruption, haughty, quarrelsome and self-assertive.[25] The biblical emphasis of the minister as exemplar of the Christian life comes through here. The aberrations that occur highlight the dangers of the leadership role, and perhaps the particular aspects of Christian virtue that the *episkopos* needs to practice. The practice of a good Christian life and virtue is still the backbone of the spirituality of the *episkopos*.

Speaking of the period from 70–200 AD, Mitchell says:

> During this period we witness the emergence of bishops and deacons as functional ministers in virtually all the churches. "Presbyter", on the other hand, seems to remain primarily a "status-title" for those in the community who are acknowledged as God-given exemplars worthy of imitation. They constitute primarily a "hierarchy" of prestige based on fruitfulness of life and maturity of conversion, though some presbyters doubtless functioned as episcopal or diaconal ministers.[26]

The *presbyteroi* had come to be council, a *presbyterum*, around the bishop. The apostolic tradition of Hippolytus suggests that the role of the presbyter was to provide pastoral advice to the *episkopos*, though at times they could be delegated to do some of the things normally done by the *episkopos*.[27] Gradually, however, they came to be removed from this counseling role, to one of leadership and liturgical activity in the outer regions of the bishop's domain. They were not required to be full time, as were the bishop and the deacons, and probably continued to carry on their family and career life, while performing their roles at the Sunday meetings of the community.[28] It was their exemplary life within the community that was the basis of their selection as *presbyteroi*. Their spirituality then was not yet determined by their ministerial role, and even that ministerial role was still developing. However it is clear that their spirituality remains rooted in the exemplary living of the Christian life important in the New Testament understanding of ministry. The comments of Origen show that the *presbyteroi* had become a privileged class within the community and suggest that the practice of the basic Christian virtues was a necessary prerequisite for their role.[29]

Even though aspects of the role of the *presbyteroi* will develop, the relationship to the bishop is an ongoing part of the development. However, it is interesting to note that after the fifth or sixth centuries, the focus moved from the *episkopos* to the presbyter, so that the bishop, as bishop, is not seen as belonging to the sacrament of order. The priest became the principal embodiment of ordained ministry. Osborne suggests that

> ... in this process of development, during the Carolingian period and the early scholastic period, the focus of *sacerdos* is no longer *episkopos* as it is during 210–600, but rather the presbyter, to the extent that *episkopos* in the scholastic period is placed outside the sphere of sacred order.[30]

For the scholastics, the presbyter was the fullness of ordained ministry. It was the Second Vatican Council that brought back the emphasis on the *episkopos*, proclaiming that the *episkopos* is the fullness of ordained ministry.[31] The presbyters share in the ministry of the *episkopos*. The Council also took up again the word "presbyter", and reintroduced the concept of the presbyterate, which recalled the role of the presbyter at the end of the second century. Nevertheless it is interesting to note that for a considerable period of time the presbyter took over from the *episkopos* as the model of ordained ministry.

The early development of the presbyter as seen in relationship to the *episkopos* has influenced the life and the spirituality of the presbyter. Certainly the bishop came to have a significant role in the way presbyters lived, at least those who were diocesan priests. The relationship to the bishop came to be seen as the particular focal point round which a spirituality of ordained ministry could be developed. Obedience to the bishop could even be seen as a key virtue within the spirituality of the ordained minister.[32] The promise of obedience came to be an important focus within the ordination rite. The Second Vatican Council has brought back a renewed emphasis on seeing the presbyter in terms of the bishop. This will surely affect future understanding of ordained ministry and the spirituality associated with it. However, it would be interesting to reflect on whether the ministry of the presbyter could be seen as a ministry in its own right. Just as the ministry of the laity has emerged from being a share in the ministry of the bishop to being a consequence of their baptism, perhaps the ministry of the presbyter may one day be again seen as a ministry in its own right.

THE ORDAINED MINISTER AS CLERIC

The clericalization of ordained ministry influenced the way the fathers spoke about ordained ministry. It was a development which set the ordained minister more and more apart from the rest of the community, and established him in a clerical state which becomes more and more important for his spirituality.

Clearly there were leadership roles within the early church, and leaders had a special role within the community. However, this distinction was to so develop that in the Middle Ages it became a division of the church into two orders, the *ordo clericorum* and the *ordo laicorum*. It also created a situation where the ordained ministry became no longer just the exercise of a particular function within the community, but a way of life, to which one committed oneself irrevocably.

In the writings of Origen, it is clear that the ordained ministers had come to be seen as a special, privileged group within the church; one which people could seek for the privileges rather than the ministry itself. By the time of Hippolytus, Christian ministry had become canonically and liturgically institutionalized. His *Traditio Apostolica* bears witness to this. The language of ordination had emerged in the writings of Tertullian, but the concept was somewhat different from what was to emerge later. For Tertullian, the ordination was the rite associated with the receiving of a mandate from the people. It was the latter that was the real focus, and the important thing, the rite was secondary.[33] However, as it developed, the rite became the focus, and the mandate was seen to come from the rite, rather than the community. The emphasis on the rite itself was to make it the instrument of separation of the ordained minister from the people. It was later to be seen to bring about an ontological change within the minister, a consecration of his very being. This is already hinted at in Cyprian's teaching that the ordained minister is holy, and that it would be sacrilegious to strike him.

It was particularly in the fourth century that the movement towards clericalization gathered momentum. The incorporation of Christianity into the Roman Empire meant that the clergy was transformed into a type of civil service with political and economic privileges of rank and status, with exemption from military service, from subjection to civil courts, and from taxation. This acquisition of civil power and privilege from the emperors clearly separated the clergy from the people and began to affect the way they saw their ministry, and the life they associated with it.[34] They became state officials. The exemption of ordained ministers from the law of the state tended to put them more under the jurisdiction of the church, so that the lives of ordained ministers came to be much more regulated by the church.

In the fifth century, the clergy began to wear special clothing outside the liturgy, which distinguished them from other Christians. The tonsure was introduced for the clergy about the year 400. Originally, a monastic practice, it served to set them apart and to highlight their separate status within the church. An attitude to ordained ministry in terms of priesthood further separated them from the people. Even the occupations which presbyters had formerly exercised were seen as incompatible with their ordained ministry, and they began to be supported by the contributions of the people. An emphasis in some councils on the irrevocability of the commitment to clerical life also emphasized that it was a state which was entered into, and which governed one's whole life. All of this had taken place by about 600.

The role of celibacy also influenced the development of the ordained ministry as a clerical body. While it is difficult to know when unmarried ministry had its origin, clearly by the sixth century celibacy was being demanded in a general way. Up until the end of the third century married clergy were the rule rather than the exception. The *episkopos* was a family man, whose relationship to his family was meant to be a model for his people.[35] The early church had a great esteem for celibacy, and sexuality played an important part in second century asceticism.[36] There had been times when married men would have to leave their wives, or abstain from sexual relationships within the union. Later it was required that an ordained minister had to marry a virgin. The importance of the clericalization of ordained ministry, in this context, is that it separated the ordained ministers from a very important aspect of the life of the people, and reiterated the separation of their spirituality from that of the people.

In the Middle Ages, this division was given legal form in the distinction between the clerical and lay orders, and the Christian community came to be seen primarily in terms of this division. Under the influence of Neoplatonism, this led to a distinction between the spiritual and the temporal, between the sacred and the secular, the former being seen as the preserve of the clergy, and the latter the preserve of the laity. The growing awareness of ordained ministry as belonging to the sphere of the sacred, and the growing distancing of the sacred from the secular, meant that more and more the life of the ordained minister was removed from the life of the people and surrounded with practices that were meant to develop the sacred sphere of life.[37]

This movement to clericalization was further developed in the eleventh century by a renaissance of Roman law which detached the power of leadership from the concept of territoriality. This flowed over into the religious sphere in the distinction between power of ordination, that is the power to celebrate the eucharist and forgive sins, and power of jurisdiction, the ability to exercise this power on behalf of a particular community. Power without jurisdiction is possible, that is to say one could be an ordained minister independent of one's relationship to a particular community. Authority and power became realities in themselves, independent of any community.[38] In earlier centuries it was not possible for ordination to take place, except in relationship to a particular community. This division had important implications for the relationship of the ordained minister to the community. The people had the right of election, and of not having imposed on them a leader that they did not want. Now ordained ministry was being seen independently of the community, as a state of life, being part of a clerical body. In feudal times this led people to be ordained for the status without ever exercising ministry within a Christian community. It led to the situation in our own day when priests who have left the ministry are still seen to retain the power, even though they do not have jurisdiction to use it.

The development of the 'sacred power' concept by the

Scholastics has been one of the chief influences on the modern understanding of ordained ministry. Ministry became more and more something that belongs to a person. It was being privatized, so that even such an essentially communitarian event as the eucharist could be seen as a private celebration of the priest. The private mass became the norm for many ordained ministers. The possession of this sacred power clearly established the ordained minister as a man of the sacred. The link between community and ordained ministry had been a significant one in the early church; both for an understanding of ministry and for the spirituality associated with it. The Council of Chalcedon could not conceive of ministry without a community, and forbade ordination when it was not linked with a particular community. Even earlier, in Hippolytus, it is the community who elects the *episkopos*,[39] and Cyprian believed that the people not only had the right to choose worthy bishops, but also to reject unworthy ones.[40]

The movement to clericalization moved the ordained minister away from the simple spirituality of discipleship to a more complex one. The biblical emphasis on example to the community had given way to a special lifestyle, different from that of other believers. In the New Testament, leadership and disciples could share the one spirituality. Now the spiritualities of the two had grown apart. The ordained minister had become, by ordination, a lifelong member of a privileged, even superior, group within the community, possessing unique power and set apart from the rest of the community. He now belonged to the sphere of the sacred, whereas they, the "saints" of the New Testament, belonged to the sphere of the temporal. The introduction of celibacy had removed the ordained minister from the normal experience of family life, and his whole way of life aligned him more with the monk than the people he served. The ordained ministry, which had been rooted in the community, was now seen as a personal possession, and could be exercised independently of the community.

THE ORDAINED MINISTER AS PRIEST

A very influential development in the early Christian understanding of ordained ministry is the movement to see it in terms of priesthood; the application to it of the Greek word *hiereus*. In the earliest times, the application was made metaphorically, but gradually came to be taken literally. In the New Testament this term is not applied to any church ministry, though a few times it is applied to Christians in general.[41] It is normally used in a metaphorical and collective way.[42] Even the application to Jesus is seen more widely today as being metaphorical (see chapter 5, below). Because it had a special application in Judaism, it would have been difficult to attribute this designation to Christian ministry until a complete and definitive separation from Judaism had taken place.

It is only in the last quarter of the second century that this term came to be used more commonly as a designation for Christian ministers, and it became the primary designation of the ordained minister during the third and fourth centuries. Cyprian played a significant role in this latter stage of the development. A number of factors were involved: a growing sacrificial emphasis on the eucharist, and an increasing tendency to see the ministry of the Christian community in terms of the priesthood of the Old Testament.

Origen was not the first to apply the term *hiereus* to ordained ministry, but he was the first to theologize ministry along those lines. He brought together the apostolic and priestly understandings of the ministry.[43] It then came to be taken up in the rituals. Ordained ministry is now being seen in terms of the cultic figure of the priest. Perhaps this more than any other movement has had a lasting effect on the spirituality associated with the ordained ministry. The ordained ministers became a member of a priestly caste, a clergy which fitted into the niche of the pagan priests in the Roman empire. They came to be seen as otherworldly, cultic, liturgical figures. This facilitated the movement towards clericalization.

There is a meeting here of two streams: an emerging Christian ministry, and the designation 'priesthood' which had a tradition of its own, both pagan and Jewish.[44] The application of this designation, both in its pagan and Jewish senses, was significant in developing the Christian understanding of ordained ministry. However, it is difficult to see that this designation belongs to the very essence of ordained ministry.[45]

In fact it was probably the growing emphasis on the eucharist as sacrifice which influenced the understanding of the ordained minister in terms of priesthood. In turn, this movement to understanding ordained ministry as priesthood was instrumental in moving the focus of ministry from the community to the eucharist. Whereas in the ritual of Hippolytus little emphasis was given to the celebration of the eucharist, and more to community leadership and exemplary life, now the focus was to be on the minister as the celebrant of the eucharist. The movement is from understanding ordained ministry as community leadership to seeing it primarily as liturgical celebration.

This development was taken further by the growing present-ation of the eucharist as the center of the whole Christian mystery, round which the rest of the mystery revolved.

This emphasis gradually focused ordained ministry on litur-gical ritual, and gave less emphasis to the role of the word within it. It needed the Second Vatican Council to remind us that the preaching of the word was the first task of the ordained minister. It meant that the ordained minister became a person of the altar, who belonged within the sanctuary. The sanctuary became not just an architectural territorial designation, but a frame of mind which influenced all the relationships of the ordained minister to the people. This emphasis on liturgical role found particular expression in the seven sacraments. The emphasis on the objective effect of the sacraments led to a downplaying of the personal role of the ordained minister, and to a diminished emphasis on his own personal spirituality. The sacrament was valid despite the personal spirituality of the minister.

Cyprian's designation of the bishop, and later the presbyter, as "priest" led to the conclusion that ordained ministers were sacrosanct, holy objects, so that it was sacrilegious to hit them. The ordained minister had become something holy, something which was to inherit all of the characteristics of such holy objects from the Jewish and Christian past. There is a growing link here between the person of the minister and the action that is performed by him, between ordained minister as priest and eucharist as sacrifice. This perhaps offered some foundation to the later Scholastic theology that spoke about the ontological transformation that takes place in ordination, and which led to his spirituality as being something that flows from the ordained minister's very being, rather than from his individual personal-ity and life situation.

This emphasis on the objective holiness of the ordained minister imposed on him a responsibility to live in an appro-priate way, worthy of the action that he performs. This led to great demands of holiness and spiritual practice which were usually taken from those groups in the church which were associated with holiness, the monks, and later the religious orders. As they came to be seen as embodying the state of perfection, the onus on the ordained minister to be seen in terms of them grew, and endured until our own times.

The result of this movement to understand the ordained minister in priestly terms was complex. It emphasized further that the ordained minister was someone set apart, along the lines of the Old Testament and pagan priests. This was highlighted by the growing link between the ordained minister and the eucharist. The ordained minister was seen more in terms of liturgical leadership than community leadership. In the Dionysian theology, the eucharist was the center of the universe, and everything was seen in relationship to it. The ordained minister as the one closest to this mystery was seen to have a unique place within creation. This led to an exalted understanding of the holiness of the ordained minister, who needed to match the holiness of the mystery with which he was involved. John Chrysostom extols the purity and piety that is demanded of the priest.[46] This holiness further separated him from the people. His life began to reflect that of the monks, and the traditional pagan and Old Testament priests. This holiness came to be seen as founded, through ordination, in his very being so that he was to be respected as holy, even when his personal life and practice did not indicate such holiness. It was almost a ritual holiness, removed from the practice of life. This movement was also instrumental in perpetuating the practice of celibacy for the ordained minister.

THE ORDAINED MINISTER AS MONK

Originally, ordained ministry was not an essential part of the monastic life. The words of Cassian, "Beware of women and bishops", embody the monastic conviction that marriage and ordained ministry would undermine their monastic commitment.[47] Ordained ministry here is clearly seen as something that would draw the monk out of the monastery into a community situation. The two roles were incompatible. However, later developments were to bring about a situation where monastic life and ordained ministry could exist comfortably together within the monastery. This development had important implications for ordained ministry.

As the priest came to be seen as more and more holy, there was an obvious move to relate the ordained minister's life to that of the monk, who was seen to be the ideal of Christian holiness. If the ordained minister was to be seen in terms of exalted holiness, then it would be natural to apply to his spirituality the principles and practices of the monks who were the masters of holiness. This was carried over in later centuries to seeing consecrated religious priests as models of ordained ministry.[48] This goes beyond the biblical emphasis on the ordained minister as an example to the community. The priest is seen as being holy in a sense that goes beyond that of the ordinary believer.

An obvious example of this tendency was Augustine, who drew his priests around him to live a life of community and poverty in imitation of the early church as described by Luke. It is interesting to note that this experiment failed and Augustine abandoned the effort.[49] He is not happy about this and seems to be rather unsympathetic to those who are not willing, or able, to live with him in poverty and community. However, this failure was not to stop others trying. The reform of Gregory VII was an important effort to restore important elements of the church. However, his concept of ministry was to make it like monasticism. Like Augustine, he wanted the diocesan clergy to take a vow of poverty and to adopt monastic common life.

It is difficult to know whether to describe the coming together of ordained ministry and monasticism as the monastizing of ministry, or the sacerdotalizing of monasticism. However, the effect was the same. The influence of monastic ordained ministers was to be considerable. This movement accelerated a process already in motion: the process of privatizing and individualizing ordained ministry. The multiplication of private masses among the monks gave concrete emphasis to the idea that ordained ministry was no longer essentially linked to a particular pastoral community, as had been the emphasis in the famous sixth canon of Chalcedon. Like monasticism, ordained ministry had become a state, a way of life in itself, different from, separate from and above the state of the baptized people. The debate as to whether it was above the state of monasticism was never decisively brought to a conclusion. What is important, however, is that what began as applying the ideals of the monk to the ordained ministry had transformed the life and spirituality of the ordained minister.

In the early church, it had been baptism that marked out the "saints". As time passed, the dividing line between the sacred and the secular moved to the monks, so that the people became part of the secular and the monks became the people of the sacred. One of the effects of monastic influence on the clergy was that ordination became the dividing line between the secular and the sacred, so that the fundamental distinction became clergy and laity.[50] Ordained ministry was now a state, rather than a function to be performed for the community.

It led to an emphasis on community living, and the practice of the evangelical counsels, the vows. Poverty was given particular emphasis due to the influence of monasticism. This has affected the lifestyle of ordained ministry because the church, in whose control the life of ordained ministers rests, has always seen them and maintained them in a lifestyle characterized by simplicity and poverty. The emphasis on obedience at least assisted the concept that obedience to the bishop was an essential aspect of the spirituality of ordained ministry, and could be seen as the real core of the spirituality of the diocesan priest. The monastic vow of chastity also was a factor in the emphasis on celibacy that remained central to discussion about the lifestyle of ordained ministry. The saying of the office as part of, or as the very core of, the spirituality of ordained ministry, was influenced by monasticism. This is not to say that it came directly from monasticism, but that the influence of monasticism gave it more impetus, and ensured that it remained an important part of the spirituality of ordained ministry. Monasticism also ensured that the liturgical role of the ordained minister would remain central. It also cemented the idea of the ordained minister as called to a high degree of holiness, and therefore that his life and spirituality would be drawn from the lives of those who were especially associated with holiness, that is to say the monks and later the religious, rather than from the lives of the believers whom he served.

CONCLUSION

The evolution of the understanding of ministry was shaped by historical situations, particular needs of the community, and different theological insights. However, the contributions of all of these influences created an understanding of ministry that had ceased to evolve, ceased to be open to the unfolding life of the church. It had come to be an ontological reality, whose being and essence had become irrevocably fixed and which was thus closed to new insights. Perhaps, in the changing ecclesial and theological situation of our own times, ministry can be freed to be influenced and shaped by the contemporary needs, as it has been in the past. To cling unnecessarily to the past is to close ourselves to the present. A relevant embodiment of ordained ministry for our own age and culture cannot be deduced from the past. What is essential to it may be deduced from the past, but its shape, its spirituality, the way it is lived must come from the present, in order to offer a meaningful proclamation and service to it.

This chapter is not meant to be simply an historical one. Its focus is ordained ministry today, and the spirituality associated with it. The importance of understanding the influences that have shaped ordained ministry and its spirituality is to appreciate what they would be like if we were to remove the effects of these influences. I believe that the various movements and models of the past are being questioned today, as new movements influence our thinking. These influences are such that they certainly make us reassess the understanding of ministry and its spirituality as it has come down to us.

Today there is a diminishing emphasis on the ordained minister as cultic priest, and on the eucharist as sacrifice; and a greater emphasis on word and community as the central focus of ordained ministry rather than the eucharist. Ordained ministry is being seen as belonging to the community rather than as a personal possession of the minister. There is a shift from the Scholastic emphasis on power to the patristic emphasis on service to the community, and from the Scholastic ontological understanding to the biblical concept of function within the community. We are experiencing a new understanding of the church and the role of ministry within it, as well as a re-evaluation of the role of the laity in the church, which is causing us to reflect further on their relationship to the ordained minister. Today, holiness is not seen as demanding separation from the world, but as able to be lived to the full in any Christian way of life; it is identified much more with the baptismal life of the believer than with any post-baptismal vocation. Part of this new approach to holiness is a new understanding of the sacred and the profane, the spiritual and the temporal. All of these movements are motivating us to re-evaluate the meaning of ordained ministry, its role in the community, and the spirituality that is to be associated with it.

In the sixteenth century, the Protestant reformers set out to re-evaluate ordained ministry in a situation that showed some similarity to our own. They rejected several of the key models within the tradition: the ordained minister as priest, cleric and monk. They rejected the association between celibacy and ordained ministry, and highlighted the importance of the laity within the Christian community. They took as their model the minister as pastor and focused their re-appraisal around the relationship of the minister to the community. They did not necessarily succeed in moving totally away from the movements to which they were reacting, but their efforts do offer some precedent for what needs to be done today.

One constant in the tradition of ordained ministry is the importance of the personal holiness of the minister. Originally this holiness was that of the "saints", the Christian believers, but unfortunately, it came to be seen in otherworldly terms. It pointed to a life beyond that of the ordinary believer, and came to be associated with models which emphasized its essentially different, separate and unique status. Perhaps, in the light of the modern recognition of the universal call to holiness, the spirituality associated with ordained ministry could look again to those "saints" from whom it took its original spirituality, the believing community. In an age when holiness is seen as stemming principally from baptismal commitment, able to be lived fully in any Christian way of life, and belonging more to the person than the office, it would be possible for the spirituality associated with the ordained minister to be more associated with that of his fellow believers. Christian discipleship could again be the model for the spirituality of the ordained minister.

A return to this model could well mean that, in terms of spirituality, primacy should be given to the minister rather than to ministry. Ministry only exists in a person, and the foundation of that ministry will be the personal faith life of that person. It is this baptismal commitment that should already be mature and proven when the believer comes to ordained ministry and which should be the foundation of the spirituality of ordained ministry. If ministry is a service within every community throughout the world, its embodiment will need to be affected by the particular culture within which it is exercised. No one spirituality of ministry will ensure this. What can ensure it is that ministry be exercised by mature Christian believers, who will bring to the ministry a shape that will make it more meaningful to the people of their community. This points to a diversity of spiritualities rather than one, or perhaps just different embodiments of the one spirituality, that of Christian discipleship.

[1]D Walker, "Spirituality and Ministry", *Challenges to Ministry*, Catholic Institute of Sydney, Sydney, 1989, 62–74
[2]Paul VI, *Evangelii Nuntiandi*, par. 4
[3]JG Dunn, *Unity and Diversity in the New Testament: An Enquiry into the Character of Earliest Christianity*, SCM Press, London, 1977, 103–123
[4]*1 Cor* 11:1
[5]*1 Cor* 4:16–17
[6]Cf. *1 Thess* 5–8; *Phil* 3:17; *Gal* 4:12; *1 Cor* 4:16–17; 11:1
[7]*1 Tim* 1:15–16; *2 Thess* 3:7–9; *1 Pet* 5:2–3; *Heb* 13:7–8
[8]*1 Tim* 15:16; *Heb* 13:7
[9]*2 Thess* 3:7–9
[10]*Phil* 3:17
[11]*1 Pet* 5:2
[12]*1 Pet* 5:3
[13]*Mk* 10:43–45
[14]*Jn* 13:14
[15]*1 Cor* 23–25; 31–33; *Rom* 15:1–2
[16]*Gal* 5:16–26
[17]*Rom* 12:3
[18]*1 Cor* 13:3–8; *Col* 3:12–17
[19]E Schillebeeckx, *Ministry: A Case for Change*, SCM Press, London, 1981, 14

[20]K Osborne, *Priesthood: A History of the Ordained Ministry in the Roman Catholic Church*, Paulist Press, New York 1988, 162

[21]*1 Tim* 3:1–13

[22]R McBrien, *Ministry: A Theological and Pastoral Handbook*, Harper and Row, San Francisco, 1987, 33

[23]G Tavard, *A Theology of Minister*, Michael Glazier, Wilmington, 1983, 119

[24]Op. cit., n. 20 above, 129

[25]H Von Campenhausen, *Ecclesiastical Authority and Spiritual Power in the Church of the First Three Centuries*, Stanford University Press, Stanford, 1969, 252–3

[26]N Mitchell, *Mission and ministry. History and theology in the sacrament of Order*, Michael Glazier, Wilmington, 1982, 199

[27]J Moehler, *The Origin and Evolution of the Priesthood*, Society of St Paul, Staten Island, 1969, 53

[28]Op. cit., n. 20 above, 124

[29]Op. cit., n. 25 above, 252–3

[30]Op. cit. n. 20 above, 160

[31]Vatican II, *Decree on the Bishop's Pastoral Office in the Church*, par. 15

[32]G Aschenbrenner, "A Diocesan Priest's Obedience", Human Development, Vol. 10, No. 2, 1989, 32–38

[33]Op. cit., n. 26 above, 231

[34]A Lemaire, *Ministry in the Church*, SPCK, London, 1977, 57

[35]Op. cit., n. 27 above, 92–93

[36]V Deprez, "Christian Asceticism Between the New Testament and the Beginning of Monasticism; The Second Century", *The American Benedictine Review*, Vol. 42, No. 2, 1991, 163–178

[37]Op. cit., n. 22 above, 38

[38]Op. cit., n. 19 above, 55–56

[39]Op. cit., n. 27 above, 510

[40]Op. cit., n. 26 above, 232

[41]"a royal priesthood" *1 Pet* 2:9, cf. *Rev* 1:6 "kingdom of priests", 5:10 "priests for our God", 20:6 "priests of God and Christ"

[42]Op. cit., n. 22 above, 31

[43]J Pelikan, *The Emergence of the Catholic Tradition*, University of Chicago Press, Chicago, 1971, 59

[44]R Hanson, *Christian Priesthood Examined*, Lutterworth Press, London, 1976, 98

[45]D Walker, "Is Ministry Essentially Priestly", *The Australasian Catholic Record*, Vol. 57, No. 2, 1989, 107–116

[46]John Chrysostom, *On the Priesthood*, 3, 4–6

[47]John Cassian, *The Twelve Books of the Institutes of the Coenobia*, ch. 18

[48]J O'Malley "Diocesan and Religious Models of Priestly Formation: Historical Perspectives", ed. Robert Wister, *Priests: Identity and Ministry*, Michael Glazier, Wilmington, 1990, 54–70

[49]Augustine, Sermon 355

[50]Op. cit., n. 19 above, 56

TWO

Priesthood in the
Middle Ages

Edmund Campion

for Emeritus Professor Jim Griffin

The Lord deprived bishops of sons; so the Devil gave them
nephews.—Pope Alexander III

I

The history of priesthood in the Western church is the history
of the mass. At its deepest level the Christian community is a
eucharistic people. Because the soundest Christian emotion is
gratitude, everything starts and ends in the mass. So that if, by
some trick of the imagination, the eucharistic element were
removed, the church would disappear.

Since worship is this foundational fact of Christian existence,
every element in the history of the church draws its meaning, in
some way or other, from its relation to the eucharist. Even
historic realities which at first glance seem merely economic or
legal—say, tithes or church courts—can be tracked back to the
mass. This does not deny their everyday economic or legal
reality; but it sets such realities in a wider frame of understanding. It gives them a reference in a bigger picture than mere
economics or law and so makes them more comprehensible
because it reveals more about them.

The politics of church life shows this clearly. Who decides
what shall be done about the public life of a community—that
is what politics is about. In the earliest Christian communities such decisions were taken communally. In those small
churches, members knew each other personally. Face to face,
they had no need of titles; first names were enough for them.
Even so, the leaders of such communities were those to
whom Jesus had said, "Do this in memory of me". And after

21

them, leadership passed to those appointed to keep him in memory.

It is important to notice that the "in memory" enjoined was *eucharistic*, not merely *nostalgic*. Their way of keeping him "in memory" was to hold a eucharist. The community prayers that have survived from the earliest church (as in the *Didache*) are eucharistic prayers: "We give thanks... We give thanks... We give thanks... " With the growth in numbers and the settling down of the Christian people, this element became more prominent. The lay philosopher Justin's account of Sunday worship in Rome about the year 150 highlights this. He described how bread along with wine mixed with water was brought forward. Over them thanksgiving prayers were said, to which the whole assembly gave its assent by saying "Amen". Justin's account is precious because it gives for the first time the lineaments of Sunday worship as it is still known throughout the Catholic world: scripture readings, homily, prayers of the faithful, offertory, eucharistic prayer, the great Amen, holy communion (including communion of the sick) and even a collection. As a layman, Justin carefully noted the role of the laity in the Sunday eucharist.

He also gave evidence of the growth of political structures within the Christian community. In particular, he noticed the importance of a man whom he called the president. While his was clearly a community of worshippers, just as clearly it was led in its worship by the president. He was the one who preached on the scripture readings. He was the one who received the offertory gifts and said over them eucharistic prayers "as much as in him lies". He was even the one to whom the collection was given to be distributed to those in need. So the president of the eucharist was also the president of the local community; he not only led its prayers, he also controlled its teaching and he oversaw its practical arrangements. Nevertheless, he acted within a body with a strong sense of community; he was inside the church, not over it.

By Justin's time, a useful word had appeared in the Christians' vocabulary: clergy. Writing from Rome to the Corinthians about the year 100, Clement had used this word to describe the leadership group in the Corinthian church. The root of this Greek word means *the chosen*: by "clergy", Clement meant those chosen from among the Christian people to lead them. Another useful Greek word then coming into currency was "bishop", meaning the principal cleric who had oversight of the whole community. Clergy and bishops were liturgically-based functionaries. They were chosen for service of the altar, as surviving ordination rites attest. By contrast, there was no ordination rite for the order of widows, according to the *apostolic tradition*, because the order had no liturgical function.

As one would expect, the history of the mass rite exhibits the same opening up of a divide between clergy and the rest of the Christian people. What had begun as a distinction of roles within a single offering community became, in time, a chasmic division between offerers (clergy) and spectators (laity). Eastern Christianity had led the way in separating clergy from laity by rich vestments, inaudible prayer and concealing iconostasis. In the West, the story was similar, if somewhat delayed. The Roman liturgy, which emphasized the role of the pope, became the pattern liturgy for the West. In time, vestments, architecture, an inaudible ritual and even the kind of bread in use would detach the mass from its origins as a communitarian prayer. Helping this process along was the need to combat Arianism in the newly Christian barbarian lands of the West. Since Arianism emphasized the humanity of Christ, its Roman opponents were at pains to stress his divinity. The mass, which made Christ present among his people, became a locale of the numinous, heavy with divine otherness, even awesome or terrible. It was best left in the hands of those specially chosen, the clergy.

Changes in thinking kept pace with such handovers to the clergy. Christians believed that Christ was present in the eucharist—but how? The development of sacramental theology came to favor a literal, material presence, which emphasized the identity between Christ's presence in the eucharist and his historical presence in Palestine in the first century. Again, the need to combat heresy helped this process along. Albigensians did dirt on the fleshly and carnal. To rebut them, Catholics underlined the physicality of the incarnation. God had taken flesh; not only that, substantially the same flesh which he had taken in the incarnation is really present to us in the eucharist. The twelfth century Royal Portal of Chartres cathedral is heavy with such incarnational–sacramental theology.

II

Changes in the mass went hand in hand with such developing theology. Since Christ was really present in the eucharistic species, they demanded utter reverence. Bread fragments and crumbs presented particular challenges to the reverent mind. So, from the ninth century, everyday baker's bread was no longer used at mass. Instead, white unleavened communion hosts came into fashion. Since these did not go stale as quickly as baker's bread, they could be divided before mass, thus diminishing the importance of the bread-breaking ceremony. Individual communion hosts also made unnecessary the friendly old communion platters which had pointed towards communal sharing. Now all that was needed was a little plate for the priest (the paten) and a vessel to hold the hosts. Nor were the hosts any longer placed in the communicants' hands; now they were placed on the tongue.

Some centuries later, theological developments stressed that the total Christ was present in either species, bread or wine. Coupled with a concern about accidental spilling, this led to the denial of the chalice to the laity; by the twelfth century even intinction was forbidden. There were exceptions to this rule; by and large, however, from the high Middle Ages the laity took communion only in wafer form. In time, people would kneel, not stand, to receive communion. Finally, the communion rail would give architectural expression to this liturgical division between the people and their priests.

The changes evidenced in the mass could be seen outside the churches also. In 321, Constantine had recognized the centrality of the eucharist in the Christian cosmology by making Sunday, the traditional day for mass, a public holiday. He also reinforced the speciality of the mass clergy by granting them favors: dispensation from civil and military service, tax exemptions, free public transport, land and building grants and enhanced social ranking. The same process of special treatment for the clergy can be observed in the Anglo-Saxon kingdoms from the arrival of Augustine of Canterbury early in the seventh century. In court, a bishop ranked equally with a king. Church property was given special protection in law, as were the clergy. Tithes and other clerical charges, such as burial fees and Peter's Pence, were enforced by law. Thus the status of the clergy as a separate class was enhanced. The effect on the clergy's mentality was almost inevitable. They came to feel and act as a special class of Christians bonded together by self-interest. This is what is known as clericalism. The Law of the Northumbrian Priests from its opening sentence gives evidence of how far the process had advanced by the early eleventh century: "If anyone offer wrong to any priest, all his colleagues are to be zealous about obtaining compensation with the help of the bishop; and in all legal matters they are to be, as it is written, of one heart and soul". *Contra mundum*—the clergy stands united in protection of their own interests, a powerful exemplar of the mentality we call clericalism.

A twelfth century dispute showed how far this clerical

privilege could be taken. When King Henry II and Archbishop Thomas Becket had their falling-out, the nub of the dispute was the right of the clergy to be tried solely in their own courts. Being a centralizer, Henry was anxious to weaken the mini-kingdom of the church (which is why he had made his friend Becket Archbishop of Canterbury). In earlier times a custom had prevailed whereby a cleric accused of a serious crime would be brought to the royal court. There he might plead clerical privilege and so be taken to the episcopal court, by a royal officer. If found guilty in the episcopal court he would be degraded, that is, reduced to the lay state. Now a layman, the ex-cleric would be taken back to the royal court for punishment, which might be death or mutilation. Such had been the custom-ary procedure; but in the reign before Henry's, known as the Anarchy of King Stephen, it had somewhat fallen into disuse. Therefore in his Constitutions of Clarendon (1164), Henry reasserted an old, but now challenged, royal right: "If the cleric be convicted or shall confess, the church ought no longer to protect him". Against this the archbishop asserted that to allow it would punish the criminous clerk twice—making him a lay-man was one punishment, death or mutilation was a second; and God (he now quoted St Jerome) did not judge anyone twice for the same offense. Becket's stand dragged contemporary canonists to his side of the argument, including the great lawyer Pope Alexander III. Hereafter, the right of the clergy to their own courts on all matters (the *privilegium fori*) was established. A significant spin-off was the growth of the papacy as the central court of appeal in church law. Nothing helped this more than the eagerness of English churchmen to appeal to Rome: of 424 decretals surviving from Alexander III's pontificate, 219 went to England. In many ways, the medieval papacy was a creation of the *Ecclesia Anglicana*. Thus the clerical order became the first multinational corporation in European history.

Clerical privileges carried a reverse side—prohibitions. In their own way, prohibitions reinforced negatively the clerical-ism fleshed out by privileges. Thus a cleric was forbidden by church law from practicing surgery, engaging in trade or the money market, going to war, participating in ordeals where blood was spilt, or hunting and hawking. (The blood prohibition looked back to the pacifism of early Christians; medieval bishops, such as Bishop Turpin in the *Song of Roland*, went into battle carrying a mace rather than a sword: contentious bishops did not spill your blood, they bashed your brains out.) Clerics were ordered to keep out of pubs and away from singsongs, actors, jesters and minstrels. They were warned against going into taverns for a meal and getting drawn into a drinking school, where they might have to shout their round, which could lead, in the knowing words of the Fourth Lateran Council, to "exile of the mind". If an honest man asked them to a tavern for a meal and lewd songs or off-color jokes started there, they were told that they should show their disapproval by not laughing. They must keep their hair tonsured and not nourish its growth, so that everyone would know that they were clerics. Unlike Benedictines or Franciscans, the secular clergy did not wear special uniforms. Nevertheless, they were commanded to wear clothes that were drab and footwear that was unfashionable. In all of these ways the clergy were marked out from their fellow Christians as a separate and distinct caste.

III

One thing in particular singled the clergy out from other Christians: they should not marry. The history of compulsory clerical celibacy has been studied exhaustively. Chiefly, however, this has been drawn from non-English sources. To right this unbalance, what follows is done from a study of English ecclesiastical sources from the ninth to the thirteenth centuries. As a historical source, synodal decrees and legal judgments are to be preferred to the racy journalism of such writers as Gerald of Wales.

Although clerical celibacy had been a feature of church life since earliest times, its espousal was by no means universal. Clerical marriage was condemned again and again; but the frequency of the condemnation shows that the practice did not disappear immediately it was condemned. In a letter to King Alfred in 890, for example, Archbishop Fulk of Rheims had praised royal opposition to such marriages, thereby giving us evidence of the continuance of these marriages. Writing at the end of the tenth century, Aelfric recorded the arguments of those who wanted priests to marry. It was, they said, an old custom among them; and, anyway, St Peter and priests of the Old Testament had wives. Some said simply that they could not live without a woman. Aelfric firmly rebutted such arguments, taking his stand on the law. Since the Council of Nicea (325), he claimed, only a priest's mother, sister or aunt had been allowed to live in his house. As for St Peter and the other apostles—they had abandoned their wives when called to the apostolate. Old Testament priests had not offered mass. Celibates had become spiritual eunuchs "for the kingdom of heaven" (*Matthew* 19:12), a sacrifice to God, as Christ had asked. Those who broke the law would be excommunicated and forfeit their orders. Aelfric's letters bear valuable witness to contemporary tensions.

At about the same time, at the other end of England, the Law of the Northumbrian Priests gives linguistic evidence of such contemporary tensions. The law ordered: "If a priest leaves a woman and takes another, let him be anathema." Three things should be noticed: this law recognized the factual existence of clerical marriage; it acknowledged that there was something remiss about this practice; and it tried to limit the practice. The language of the Anglo-Saxon text reveals its intention: it speaks not of a "legal spouse" (wife) but of a "woman" (cwenan) whom the priest "takes" (nime) rather than "weds" (wifige). Thus its very words mirror the tension between real and ideal.

Such tension can also be read in the repetition of the ban on clerical marriage in councils and synods throughout this period. The Gregorian Reform, one of whose primary aims was the enforcement of clerical celibacy, began to make its impact on English lawbooks in the 1070s. Carriage of the Reform was entrusted to the new Norman prelates who had come in with the Conqueror—indeed, it could be read as a pay-off for papal political support of the conquest. Yet here lay a difficulty. For the Norman clergy were, in Christopher Brooke's words, "by repute among the most uxorious in Europe".[1] Brooke lists the dozen or so Norman upper clergy known to be married, including archbishops and bishops. Clerical marriage had the support of intellectuals, the most cogent of whom was the Norman "Anonymous of York"; and among the people at the grassroots, where the new papal decrees could provoke riots (the clergy wives of Normandy nearly lynched the reformer Bernard of Tiron). Widespread resistance to altering the status quo led Archbishop Lanfranc, in the first canon of his primatial Council of Winchester (1076), to allow married parish clergy to keep their wives, enjoining only that in future candidates for priesthood or diaconate must make previous profession that they were not married. A later Archbishop of Canterbury, Anselm of Bec, closed this loophole in 1102: no archdeacon, priest, deacon or canon was to marry or, if married, retain his wife; candidates for ordination would order all women, other than the Nicene near relatives, from priests' homes. His letters, however, reveal that there was considerable non-compliance with these orders. Nevertheless, the reformers were beginning to make an impression.

The First Lateran Council (1123) is a significant landmark for it not only forbade matrimony to clerics in higher orders, it also declared that any such attempted marriage was to be broken.

The Second Lateran Council (1139) reinforced that by making clerical marriage not only illegal but invalid. After 1123, then, it became clear that marriage would be a severe impediment to promotion in the church. So it proved. The Council of Westminster in 1127 decreed that clerics were not to share their quarters with women and the parish priests who clung to their concubines or wives (Latin: *concubinis (quod absit) vel forte coniugibus adheserint*) should be deprived of their benefices and thrown out of the parish. This was almost the last time the old terminology was used in English laws. Hereafter, the women in question were called, not wives, but concubines or fornicators (*fornicariae*). Such language reflected growing legal stringency as well as a developing theology of matrimony. Even so, the familiar gap between theory and practice may still be evidenced, as in the *Anglo-Saxon Chronicle*'s account of the national council at London in 1129:

> It turned out to be all about archdeacons' wives and priests' wives, that they were to give them up by St Andrew's Day, and anyone who would not do so, should forgo his church and his house and his home, and nevermore have a claim to them. This was ordered by William of Canterbury, the archbishop and all the diocesan bishops that were in England, and the king gave them all permission to go home, and so they went home, and all the orders availed nothing— they all kept their wives by permission of the king, as they had done before.[2]

As the *Chronicle* suggests, apart from public opinion, the only coercive force at the church's disposal was the power of the king. One might buy his acquiescence by paying a fine. That had happened before; it happened in 1129; and it could happen again. A century later, one of King John's replies to the Interdict (1208-1214) was to distrain those women he called with rough royal humour, the *sacerdotissae*, leaving their consorts the choice of ransoming them or abandoning them.

By the beginning of the thirteenth century, however, the picture had changed. Those gentlemen's clubs of the English clergy, the cathedral chapters, had been monasticized; thus making hereditary canonries a thing of the past. By then, there were many more monks and monasteries in England, a pointer to popular spirituality and, it may also be, public opinion. Whatever about the parish clergy—and for the most part they are lost to our sight—for half a century the higher clergy had eschewed matrimony, showing an increasing respect for law, which was a concomitant of rising educational levels. The new theology of marriage may have had something to do with it too:

honeyed words could not disguise the fact that the best a clergyman could offer a girl was only second best to a recognized marriage. Negatively, the law pursued the clergy's consorts. They were to be expelled from the parish house; nor could the priest keep them elsewhere. They were to be whipped (Statutes of Winchester 1224) and excommunicated and no one should offer them hospitality. When they died, they were to be buried without rites. They might even (Diocese of Wells 1258) be handed over to the secular arm for punishment. The problem would not go away. Yet by the end of the thirteenth century, judging by its less frequent appearance in synodal decrees and canons, it was being contained.

By then, too, thinking about the mass had changed. When Archbishop Stephen Langton returned from exile in 1213, he showed what ideas he had absorbed in the reform circles he had been frequenting on the Continent. The statutes for the Diocese of Canterbury, which he then issued, were a prolegomenon to the greatest ecumenical council of the Middle Ages, the Fourth Lateran Council. Many of the distinctive reform ideas of this Council got an early airing in the Canterbury statutes. The elevation of the host after the consecration, for example, had begun in Paris only in very recent years. Archbishop Stephen enjoined it on his diocese and ordered that every church should possess "a Canon of the mass corrected according to Canterbury usage, so that the words of the Canon at mass might be said loud and clear". Since time immemorial, the canon had been recited aloud; it was a legacy of the mass as a communal offering and the church as a community of offerers, a harking-back to Justin and Rome in 150 AD. Yet, even as Langton wrote, avant-garde liturgists in Paris were beginning to drop their voices as they began the canon. Theirs was the liturgy of the future, the "blessed mutter of the mass" and all that. The liturgical modernism of the silent-canon men was closely linked to the new theology of the eucharist, then emerging in Paris, which would receive its lapidary enunciation in the work of Thomas Aquinas. The feast of Corpus Christi, celebrated from about 1230 and extended to the universal church in 1264, was an impression of the same theological movement. What the new men were stressing was the corporeality of Christ's presence in the eucharist, a follow-on of the doctrine of transubstantiation defined as *de fide* by the Fourth Lateran Council.

This insistence that the body "born" on the altar was the same body born to the Virgin Mary had powerful links to the celibacy question. Just as Mary was a virgin, so too the priest should be not only chaste but also unmarried. Everything surrounding the very body of Christ must be special, separate. Two centuries earlier, Aelfric had allowed chalices of glass or tin, as well as gold or silver; now, only precious metal would do. Langton had told his parish priests to reserve the blessed sacrament in a clean pyx, which would in time be suspended over the altar; by 1281 another Archbishop of Canterbury, John Pecham, would order reservation in a tabernacle.

As the eucharist, so the priest. The long development of the mass had seen him change from spokesman of the offering community to representative of the God who bestowed himself as gift. Catholic liturgy balances the tensions between transcendence and immanence, putting its weight now here, now there. So too the priest is drawn now one way, now the other. By the thirteenth century the liturgy was heavily transcendental; and consequently the priest's lifestyle was separated from the normal experiences of the quotidian world. So it would remain, until changes in theology and liturgy began to move the balance in the opposite direction.

---

[1]Cf. Christopher N L Brooke, *The Idea of Medieval Marriage*, Oxford University Press, New York, 1989

[2]Cf. *The Anglo-Saxon Chronicle: A Revised Translation*, eds. D Whitelock et al., Greenwood Press, Westport Conn., 1986

THREE

From "Clerk-in-orders" to "Pastoral Minister"—the Reformation of Ordained Ministry

William Wright

The trouble with the ordained ministry in the fifteenth century was that there wasn't one. Of ordained priests there were plenty, indeed far too many, but of the notion that there should be a particular ministry attached to ordination we see little evidence. Huge slices of the male population were in holy orders for one reason or another, yet this mass of clergy provided only a barely adequate pastoral ministry, and the demand for something better was growing.

By the end of the sixteenth century Europe had decided on the form of that "something better": men were to be ordained for a ministry as preachers and pastors or, if they could not or would not perform that ministry, not ordained at all. The century that witnessed the Reformation reshaped the rationale of ordination. Where the medieval church had consecrated the person of the cleric and left open to him a myriad of possible functions, the early modern church consecrated *a function*: the Protestant minister and the Counter-Reformation priest were to be teachers and models to a laity that was in their care; they were to be what we call "clergymen".

I

It is perhaps necessary to begin this account of that change by stressing the number and diversity of priests in the fifteenth century. In most parts of Europe there was probably a local

31

priest assigned for every two or three hundred people. In addition to these there were the monks who, since the tenth century, were normally priests. The ranks of these "regular clergy" had also been swollen since the thirteenth century by the success first of the canons and then of the mendicant orders, the friars. But, as Edmund Campion has it in his chapter of this volume, "the history of the priesthood is the history of the mass", and the really dramatic growth in the numbers of priests at the end of the Middle Ages was the product of changed views of the mass.

As the penitential discipline of the church, driven by the Crusade indulgence and the trauma of the Black Death, concentrated more and more on the remission of the sufferings of the souls in purgatory, so the mass became less a communal rite, less even an occasion for the miracle of Christ's presence in the host, and more and more a sacrifice offered for the living and (especially) the dead.

Throughout Europe in the fifteenth century there grew up confraternities, guilds, chantries and other foundations whose sole or main purpose was to provide for masses to be sung for their members' dead. These lay groups employed salaried priests outside the parish system, and outside the religious orders, simply to perform these services. These greatly swelled the ranks of priests who had little or no pastoral responsibility.

Finally, too, there were all those who entered holy orders for career reasons that had little to do with religion, let alone ministry. Younger sons of great families found bishoprics, abbacies and deaneries an accessible route to the wealth, status, lifestyle and political clout of which the law of primogeniture might otherwise deprive them. And for the bright sons of merchants and even lesser folk, the path to education, and the possibility of rising through the ranks of the burgeoning bureaucracies, lay either through the law or the church. This choice is explicit in the lives of many of the great figures of the sixteenth century: Luther, More, Calvin and many others. And as little as we might think of their lives as "priestly", the dazzling careers of figures as diverse as Thomas Wolsey and Erasmus are scarcely conceivable had they not been qualified by ordination to receive the patronage of the church.

A priest in the late medieval church, then, might be a great minister of state or an ambassador or a lord of the manor; he might be a scholar or a secretary in some great household; he might, as a friar, be an itinerant preacher or pardoner; he might be a monk or a private chaplain; he might be in the employ of a lay organization as a singer of masses for the dead. He might even be resident in a parish, providing the pastoral ministry to the people: but if he was, he was likely to be a very lowly priest indeed.

Parish ministry tended to be in the hands of the very slightly qualified. The functions were simple and, more importantly, the income was often very low; a well-educated priest could do better. In the English diocese of Coventry and Lichfield at this time, for example, there were 210 rectories and 187 vicarages, but half to three-quarters of these had annual incomes of ten pounds or less. At that rate, so said Hugh Latimer, a parson was "not able to buy him books nor give his neighbor drink". Were the parish worth much more, it would support a learned man, but it often supported him in London or Paris or Padua, while he paid a curate actually to serve the parish.

The local priest had the not inconsiderable virtue that he tended to be a local man who shared the family connections, farming work, recreations and aspirations of the people. He was generally capable of saying mass and performing the sacraments with at least sufficient decorum, and of carrying out the many rituals of blessing. He had a special task, too, of resolving local squabbles and keeping the peace. If he had faults, they were those of his people: drinking, gaming, wenching; and the weight of evidence suggests that, at the local level, he was an accepted, if not exactly revered, institution right up to the Reformation and beyond, and that he gave general satisfaction. But despite his theoretical dignity as a consecrated person, his work was menial and had the status and income of such. His time was running out.

It was in the towns that the surfeit of priests was most evident, as well as the absence of any particular ministry attached to priesthood. At the turn of the sixteenth century the English town of Norwich, with a population of about 10,000, contained forty-six parish churches, 117 secular clergy, thirty-eight monks and 120 friars. At that rate, about one in twenty of the males of all ages was in holy orders. In the German imperial city of Worms the rate was one in ten. In London, then a city of 50,000, the number of priests is unknown, but on one occasion early in the sixteenth century more than seven hundred were counted in a single procession. Strasbourg (population 20,000) was home to six hundred priests, most of them serving its 200 altars endowed for masses for the dead. In Zurich the clergy held one third of all taxable property, and in England they held up to a third of all productive land.

The medieval church was a huge operation and, as virtually all functions in the church had been assimilated to the priesthood, it was a huge body of priests. Little wonder if a catchy little song was doing the rounds in Germany: "Priests, monks and nuns, Are but a burden to the earth". Added to the picture, the tax and legal exemptions of the clergy were sore points in many a city.

Concern about the numbers and quality of priests, however, was by no means limited to the tavern-haunters of Saxony or to budget-conscious burgesses. Erasmus' strictures on the ignorance of clergy and the venality of monks and friars are well known; but if his critique was largely moral, others of his circle saw more clearly the link between overproduction and lack of quality control. "All who offer themselves", wrote John Colet, Dean of St Paul's "are forthwith admitted without hindrance. Hence proceed those hosts both of unlearned and wicked priests which are in the church." Thomas More agreed: "...if the bishops would once take into priesthood better laymen and fewer... all the matter would be half emended". In his own *Utopia* priests were both learned and holy, and therefore very few. One English bishop was of the same mind: in Rochester only forty-four priests were ordained in thirty years. But John Fisher's exception proved the rule. Overall England continued to ordain more than five hundred priests each year right up to the Reformation in the 1530s.

Nonetheless, while ordination continued unabated, moves to secure a more adequate pastoral ministry were well under way. The Capranica was founded in Rome in 1457 to produce educated parish clergy, and the example was followed in Spain soon after. More importantly, the laity of the towns were increasingly shifting for themselves. Those same citizens of Norwich, who through their wills showered money on the chantry priests for masses for their souls, were increasingly also leaving bequests for the university education of priests. In the first decades of the sixteenth century about one will in eighteen left money for this purpose, twice the rate of the preceding half-century. The results showed. In the first half of the fifteenth century less than one in thirteen of Norwich's beneficed clergy had held a degree: in the opening decades of the sixteenth century it was nearer half.[1] Of course the greater number of priests were unbeneficed, curates or chantry priests, and of these very few were graduates, but the citizens were at least showing signs of wanting that to change.

Things had gone much further in Germany and Switzerland, where the independence of action of civic communities was much greater. Here many town corporations employed a town preacher or "people's priest", principally as a preacher. In Wurtemburg, forty-two towns had employed preachers prior to the

Reformation. Each was required to hold a degree and to preach one hundred sermons per year. In Switzerland too, of fifty-nine such civic preachers forty-six are known to have been graduates, fourteen holding doctorates of divinity. There were such preachers in most southern German towns by 1500. There were also monks, chantry priests and all the ranks of the unlettered, of course, and in their thousands, but the citizens were showing a taste for a preaching ministry in the most tangible of ways—they paid themselves for what the church did not otherwise provide.[2]

Even in England, where provision for town preachers was not far advanced, it has recently been noted that physical provision for preaching was widespread. In Devon and Cornwall, late medieval pulpits in stone or wood have been identified in at least thirty-one towns, including such insignificant hamlets that it seems likely pulpits were virtually ubiquitous on the eve of the Reformation, and that most churches had seating. These west country churches must largely have relied on the occasional sermons of passing friars, but they were already equipped for this type of ministry. Late medieval parishes were still the source of funds for mass-priests, chantries and absentees of all sorts, but they were increasingly showing a taste for a more sophisticated preaching priest as well. Very soon the Reformation theology would give them license to indulge that taste to the exclusion of all other forms of priest.

II

In virtue of a physical anointing, when their hands are consecrated, and in virtue of their tonsure and vestments, the clergy claim to be superior to the Christian laity, who, nevertheless have been baptized with the Holy Spirit. The clergy can almost be said to regard the laity as lower animals, who have been included in the church along with themselves... Now we, who have been baptized, are all uniformly priests in virtue of that very fact. The only addition received by priests is the office of preaching, and even that with our consent. (*The Babylonian Captivity of the Church*, 1520)[3]

In these characteristically vigorous phrases, Martin Luther brushed aside the medieval conception of the priest. The Reformation would know nothing of the sacrament of orders; of acting *in persona Christi*; of the indelible character; of offering sacrifice for the living and the dead. In place of the priest personally empowered to work God's mysteries, the reformers would set up the preacher, the minister of God's word.

When Luther declared "we are all uniformly priests", he intended to abolish the notion that an ordained man was different from any other Christian in his person and regardless of his occupation. He certainly did not intend to abolish a structured, official, even "ordained", ministry. Very quickly he was involved in rancorous efforts to suppress those who set themselves up as preachers. He drove out the so-called "heavenly prophets" and set himself forever against Anabaptists and all other self-appointed preachers. Common priesthood through baptism was one thing, the office of preacher in the church was another. By the time of the Augsburg Confession the Lutheran position was clear and terse: "It is taught among us that nobody should publicly teach or preach or administer the sacraments in the church without a regular call". Abolishing the priesthood as a priesthood, Luther had certainly not abolished the clerical order as a social fact. He had, indeed, more tightly specified what a minister of the church was to be: a preacher duly appointed to lead and instruct a congregation. He abolished the ordo of priests to set up what we recognize as the type of the "clergyman".

Luther himself, of course, had held the office of preacher in the Castle Church of Wittenberg. Many of those who took up and led the Reformation were also town preachers or people's priests, already fulfilling, *mutatis mutandis*, a ministry that the Reformation now made *the* ministry. The Reformation did not invent a new model of ministry; its originality lay in abolishing all other forms of priestly life. Stripped of special priestly consecration, the Protestant minister was nonetheless much the same animal sociologically as the old town preacher. His position in the town was stronger, however, in that he no longer had to compete with, or be compromised by, a host of other types of priest. His battles for leadership would henceforth be with the (also baptized) magistrates.

In getting rid of the "other" priests, the Reformation's ministry was again a reflection of developments in the view of the mass. The Augsburg Confession was at pains to assure the emperor that the Lutherans had not abolished the mass, indeed, "no conspicuous changes have been made in the public ceremonies of the mass". But, "the mass is not a sacrifice to remove the sins of others, whether living or dead, but should be a communion in which the priest and others receive the sacrament for themselves. (Therefore) other unnecessary masses which were held in addition to the parochial mass, probably through abuse, have been discontinued".

Discontinued, along with all the unnecessary masses, were,

of course, all the unnecessary priests. In place of the six hundred priests that had served its churches and chapels, reformed Strasbourg required only thirteen ministers by 1536. Significantly, eight of those preachers held higher degrees, and all but one of the total number came from outside the town. The ministry had become more "professional": their functions demanded higher qualifications, and these set them apart from parishioners, as a clerical elite, across a social and educational divide at least as significant as the old signposts of tonsure and celibacy. The new preacher might not be consecrated, he might be married, but he was clearly not just "one of us" for most of the baptized.

In England the monasteries and the chantries were dissolved and their priests decently pensioned, but the parish system was left virtually untouched. The liturgy of the Book of Common Prayer, too, could be (and was) celebrated by priests who could never have qualified as preachers on the Continent. Thus the change of model proceeded more slowly in England, to the chagrin of the more ardent spirits who came to be known as "Puritans". In effect, England was stuck in the position that the south German towns had reached fifty years earlier. English towns retained all their parish churches, where the liturgy was celebrated from the book and for low wages, but town corporations began to compete to provide large enough salaries to attract at least one learned preacher.

Exeter, for example, was lumbered with nineteen small parish churches. In Switzerland the town council would simply have suppressed many of them, but in England this required the consent of Parliament. The worthies of Exeter tried several times, but the gentry who gathered in the Commons were just the sort who gained influence from their right to appoint clergy to livings, and the moves failed. In the end the Exeter council accepted the status quo and found extra funds to appoint a town preacher in addition to the nineteen incumbents. England lived, uneasily at times, with mixed models.

Gradually, ever so gradually, the universities would turn out enough graduates to increase the stock of learned preachers in England. But the pace was too slow for the more godly who, apart from denouncing old-fashioned vicars for their popish ways, instituted some interesting experiments in alternative ways of training, or retraining, clergy. Such were the "prophesyings" of Elizabeth's reign; "in-service days" almost, at which the learned preached to the unlearned ministers, by way of instruction and example. There was also set up a form of parallel clergy in the institution of "lecturers": preachers, often too Protestant to accept the remaining rituals of the Common Prayer, who were employed to make up for the deficiencies of local priests by giving "afternoon sermons", without episcopal ordination.

Such private initiatives of the godly were viewed with suspicion by the monarch and the bishops, and ultimately differences over the ministry were to be among the matters at issue in the Civil War. Unfortunately for the respectable godly, the final seizure of power by the army gave license to all manner of popular preaching, the equivalent of Luther's heavenly prophets. Ranters, Shakers, Quakers, Seekers, and others, were certainly not the "correct" model of Protestant learned clergyman, but it took the return of the king and bishops to restore religious order. In England, then, the triumph of the respectable, learned, preaching clergyman was delayed until the eighteenth century.

Before leaving England, and with it the account of the new paradigm of ordained ministry in its Protestant form, it is necessary to note one other feature of that model which will also be evident in Catholic lands. The initial call for a new type of ordained minister, which took place well before the Reformation, had been a call not only for increased learnedness but also for improved morals.[4] The contraction of the body of clergy to an educated few in Continental Protestantism had secured one pillar of the new structure, but it was no guarantee of the other. There can be no certainty that an educated man will be more virtuous than an unlettered one, or, for that matter, any more possessed of pastoral skills. Luther had been embarrassed by the moral failures of some of his ministers, and had himself given offense to some by his drinking, intemperate language, and tendency to support his princes right or wrong. This was not how a Genevan minister conducted himself.

In Geneva, Calvin had famously tried to reform the manners of an entire community, closing down the taverns, regulating dress styles, even prescribing the admissible size of meals. This did not prevent his being compromised by the adultery of his son-in-law and the larceny of his personal servant. How was a morally irreproachable ministry to be secured? And who, in Professor Chadwick's happy image, would teach doctors of divinity how not to drop the baby at the font?[5]

In Geneva they tried self-regulation. Once a quarter, the ministers gathered to correct each other's faults. But in England experiments were made in providing actual moral and pastoral training for candidates for ministry. These again were private initiatives. In northern England, Bernard Gilpin attached to a grammar school a residence for up to twenty candidates for ministry, where they were taught and trained under his godly eye. In the 1580s a conference of puritan ministers resolved that each of them should take under his wing a candidate who, already having his degree, needed to be instructed in his duties. And in the next century, in Essex, one puritan ex-minister spent twenty-three years taking graduates for further training, giving them "excellent advice for Learning, Doctrine, and Life". We see in these experiments the germ of an idea of training for ministry as more than mere theological education. This was the element of reform that was to be taken furthest by the Catholics.

III

An ignorant and venal clergy had been the object of reformers' attacks long before the Reformation; the institution of town preachers that most clearly shows the new demand for a learned preaching clergy happened under the auspices of the old church. But the system that produced an excess of lowly-paid, scarcely-trained priests, and placed them in closest proximity to the people, remained in place when the Reformation struck. The ignorance of the clergy handed the reformers their most potent propaganda tool. The old church, too, had finally to take into account the call for a better pastoral ministry.

The famous report on needed reforms, the *Consilium de emendanda Ecclesia*, produced by Cardinal Contarini and his colleagues in 1537, unequivocally accepted that the ignorance of many clergy was a scandal. It proposed better education as the remedy, and the matter was taken up at Trent in 1546. The Council fathers, however, looked back to the old legislation for cathedral schools and, at this stage, what had not met the need before failed to meet it again.

In 1556, however, one of the members of Contarini's committee returned to Queen Mary's Catholic England as papal legate. Cardinal Reginald Pole's attempts at reform included the enactment of a decree about training priests that included a new word: seminary. The cathedrals of England were to have schools in which boys from the age of twelve were to be educated in grammar, theology, and discipline. From this early age they would learn to rise early, hear mass daily, wear the soutane and tonsure, and eventually emerge "as from a seed-plot" (*tamquam ex seminario*) as worthy leaders of the church. The idea took on.

Back at Trent in 1563 a decree was passed, "*de seminariis*". All bishops were to set up a seminary. It was not prescribed as the only possible training for an ordinand (that would not happen until 1965), but it was to provide especially for the education of poor students, those most likely in the past to have scraped into the clergy with minimum qualifications.

Cardinal Borromeo's elaborate system of seminaries opened in Milan the next year, along with others, and the Roman seminary in 1565. The English seminary at Douai in the Spanish Netherlands perhaps went further than others in self-consciously matching the Protestants at their own game: its students were taught Hebrew and Greek and required to read the Old Testament twelve times and the New Testament sixteen times in three years. They were trained to preach in English. If Englishmen wanted a clergy to preach the Bible to them, here were Catholic priests who could do it.

Of course the Catholic reform could not simply follow the Protestant pattern, producing learned preachers and jettisoning all other types of priest. Whatever compromises Catholic theologians might be willing to make with Luther on justification and the authority of Scripture, they could not swallow his teaching that the baptized are all "uniformly priests", nor could they budge on the nature of the mass as a propitiatory sacrifice for the living and the dead. In the end, however, regarding the type of ministry exercised by Catholic priests and their position as clergy vis-a-vis the laity, these doctrinal differences came to matter surprisingly little.

On the one hand, the mainstream Protestants had kept up a real distinction between the clerical class and the people. In Protestant towns the clergy tended to rank alongside the magistracy as a parallel peak of the civic hierarchy, and everywhere the trend to intermarriage between clerical families reinforced the impression that the clergy were a group apart.

On the other hand, while Catholics maintained the propitiatory nature of the mass, in practice the bottom dropped out of the purgatory market. Luther had been far from alone in his doubts about the sale of indulgences, and that trade collapsed at the first onslaught. Mass for the dead, of course, remained, but the demand withered. Already when Queen Mary reestablished Catholicism in England, it had been notable that while the people welcomed back the saints and the ceremonies, there were fewer legacies left for masses, and almost no revivals of the chantries. The promise of salvation in exchange for cash offerings was in bad odor, and, while the doctrine remained, the popularity of the "rites of purgatory" had diminished.

Even the Council of Trent seemed a little cool on purgatory. It insisted the doctrine be taught and believed, but devoted a third of its decree on the subject to sounding cautions: " . . . things that are uncertain or have the appearance of falsehood . . . shall not be made known publicly and discussed. But those things that tend to a certain type of curiosity or superstition, or that savor of filthy lucre, they (the bishops) shall prohibit as scandals and stumbling blocks to the faithful". The days when the Catholic church could or would maintain an army of priests simply to sing for the dead were passing away. Henceforth the Catholic priest's natural function, the one for which he was now trained, would be to celebrate the liturgy in full, to preach, to instruct the faithful, to give good example in piety and morality, and to exercise pastoral care. It was much what the Protestant minister did, albeit in a different doctrinal framework.

There still remained diversity among seventeenth-century Catholic priests: there were still the monks, there were still the religious orders. Even these, however, have gradually been pressed more and more into parochial service or, in the case of newer congregations, never became orders of priests in the first place. Meanwhile the seminaries made the secular clergy more homogeneous. Educated apart, their students took on the attitudes, piety, and even the dress that the seminaries inculcated. They too became in many respects "clergymen". Even if their celibacy and their power to consecrate still invested them with the additional aura of sacred persons, they were sacred persons expected to do a job, a job that outside the Catholic church was done by Protestant ministers.

IV

John Bossy, in his little book, *Christianity in the West 1400-1700*, has proposed that a sea change overtook Western Christianity between the fifteenth and seventeenth centuries, and that, with differing nuances, both Protestantism and Tridentine Catholicism are children of that change.[6] In Bossy's account, the change was from a communal religion whose rites cemented the bonds of kinship and community, to a religion of the word, of concepts and laws which taught the individual his personal spiritual and moral responsibilities under God. The sixteenth-century demand for a preaching ministry was, for Bossy, one token of that new religion of which the ultimate symbol might be the catechism.

The matters under consideration in this chapter are much in accord with Bossy's view. There was a demand among early

modern Christians for a new type of interface between themselves and their church. They wanted a church that would speak
and instruct, a religion that could be heard and understood, and
thus made their own. It was the demand for a faith one could
hold, rather than simply belong to; and it required a ministry
that knew what that faith was about and could explain it, rather
than simply perform its mysteries on behalf of the people. It was
a demand, too, for ministers who could model Christian piety
and morality, rather than produce wonders, *ex opere operato*,
independent of their personal qualities. Somehow the state of
civic life, the development of society, had produced this demand
in Christendom. The church, and then the churches, responded
accordingly by reshaping Christian ordained ministry. The
priest, who in the Middle Ages had been consecrated to do
things for the laity that they could not do for themselves,
became (once again?) the instructor and model in a personal
Christianity which was in principle attainable by all the faithful.

[1]Cf. Norman P Tanner, *The Church in Late-Medieval Norwich 1370-1532*, Pontifical Institute of Medieval Studies, Toronto Ont., 1984
[2]Cf. Steven E Ozment, *The Reformation in the Cities: The Appeal of Protestantism to Sixteenth-
century Germany and Switzerland*, Yale University Press, New Haven, 1975
[3]Cf. *Martin Luther: Selections from His Writings*, ed. J Dillenberger, Anchor-Doubleday, New
York, 1961, 345
[4]Cf. Patrick Collinson, *The Religion of Protestants: the Church in English Society 1559-1625*,
Clarendon Press, Oxford, 1982
[5]O Chadwick, "The Seminary", *Studies in Church History, the Ministry: Clerical and Lay*, eds. W
J Shells and Diana Wood, Blackwell, Oxford, 1989
[6]J Bossy, *Christianity in the West 1400-1700*, Oxford University Press, Oxford, 1985

FOUR

Priestly Metaphors in the New Testament

Brian Byron

In this chapter I am using the term "priest" in its cultic sense, that is in the sense of the Latin *sacerdos* or the Greek *hiereus*. When dealing with priesthood in my recent book *Sacrifice and Symbol*, I took the position that in the New Testament the term "priest" is not applied to Christ and to the Christian community in a literal sense but in a metaphorical sense.[1] I have been given the opportunity to develop that thesis in more detail here.

The cultic, sacerdotal or liturgical role involved in the ordained Christian ministry is only a part of a wider reality. Collaborators in this volume deal with other aspects of this reality. Just what is the integrating or governing concept in our ordained ministry is the question of identity, which has engaged the attention of many thinkers in the latter half of this century. I do not address this issue here. I am attempting to clarify the sense which the word "priest" (*sacerdos*, not *presbyter*) and its cognates have when applied in the New Testament to Jesus, to the Christian community and to good works. I suggest that all such usages are metaphorical. Nevertheless, I will suggest that the term applies *literally* to the ordained Christian priest (episcopal or presbyteral).

I

At first sight it may seem obvious that Jesus was literally a priest, for it is clearly stated in the *Letter to the Hebrews* that Jesus is

43

a priest, indeed, a high priest (2:17; 3:1; 4:14). He is given the title of high priest by God: "Nor did Christ give himself the glory of becoming high priest, but he had it from the one who said to him: *You are my son, today I have become your father*, and in another text: *You are a priest of the order of Melchizedek, and for ever.*" (*Hebrews* 5:5–6). The treatment of Christ's priesthood and sacrifice continues, especially through chapters 7–11.

Furthermore, the assertion of Jesus' priesthood is repeated many times by the fathers of the church, by St Thomas Aquinas (see *sacerdotium* in index of *Summa Theologica*), by popes and councils, in the liturgy (votive mass of Christ the priest, the holy eucharist B, preface of Easter V, preface of mass of Chrism), and is the starting point of the encyclical of Pius XII, *Mediator Dei*.

Nonetheless, the description of Jesus as a priest by the author of *Hebrews* is metaphorical, not literal, and as all other assertions are based on *Hebrews*, they too must be understood metaphorically. Indeed the author of *Hebrews* says: "In fact, if he were on earth, he would not be a priest at all, since there are others who make the offering laid down by the Law and these only maintain the service of a model or a reflection of the heavenly realities" (8:4-5). This claim is not original to me but was made by Jerome Smith in *A Priest Forever: A Study of Typology and Eschatology in the Epistle to the Hebrews*.[2]

DIFFERENT USES OF LANGUAGE

To back up this statement it will be necessary to go into the various uses of language. Scholastics divide language into univocal, analogical and equivocal. Analogical is subdivided into proper and improper. Both proper and improper are subdivided into proportional and attributional. Improper analogy is also called metaphor. These may be defined as follows:

Univocity

Univocal language is that which is used in exactly the same sense of two different subjects: "Earth is a planet", "Saturn is a planet".

Analogy

Analogy is used when a term is used of two subjects in a way that is partly the same and partly different. This can be either by attribution or proportionality.

(a) Attribution

The first, analogy of attribution, is when a term is used with a primary reference to one subject and to other subjects in relation to the primary one. It may be exemplified: "John is healthy" and "Exercise is a healthy activity for John". The first statement describes the organism itself, the second activity that is conducive to the health of that organism.

(b) Proportionality

The second kind of analogy, proportionality, is when a term is predicated of two subjects with a different but related meaning. It can be instanced: a *good* person, a *good* plan; *catch* a ball, *catch* a train.

Sometimes it is tempting to place generic or specific predicates in this category, such as man is an *animal*, an ox is an *animal*. This has been termed "analogy of inequality" but following Aristotle the tradition accepted that this usage is reducible to univocity and the category was not retained.[3]

Proper and improper analogy or metaphor

Proper and improper analogy can be applied to either attribution or proportionality. The examples above are proper. Improper analogy is metaphor. It entails an essential leap from one thing to another, as for example "the economy is healthy" (in comparison with a *healthy* organism) would be improper analogy of proportionality, while "increase in exports is healthy for the economy" is improper analogy of attribution. This is an "improper" use of language. Indeed the essence of metaphor is that one thing is spoken of as though it were another; that is, by predicating metaphorically you are implicitly *denying* that same predication literally because you are speaking of something as though it were *other*.[4] My friend whom I uncharitably refer to as a "silly cow" is by that metaphorical assertion implied to be *not* literally a cow, otherwise he would have an excuse for being so stupid!

It is vitally important to note the difference between proper and improper analogy, between literal and figurative speech. The importance is brought out in the other method of dividing language discussed below.

There are subdivisions of metaphor such as personification and anthropomorphism. The use of animals with human foibles as in comic strips and Aesop's fables is a sort of reverse personification. The *Book of Judges* (Chapter 8) uses trees in a similar way to give a lesson on monarchy. It has been suggested by Jerome Smith (see note 2, above) that the biblical category, typology, is a metaphorical usage.

Equivocation

Equivocal terms are the same words used with completely different and unrelated meanings, for example "pen" which can mean a writing instrument or an enclosure. If equivocity is not adverted to it can cause great confusion but the concept itself presents no difficulty.

There are other ways also of classifying different uses of language. Janet Martin Soskice, for instance, first divides language into literal and figurative. For her, the literal is subdivided into univocal, analogical and equivocal, while figurative is subdivided into the various tropes: simile, metaphor, synecdoche, hyperbole and so on.

Each of these divisions has its advantages. The scholastic division illustrates the steady progression from univocity to equivocation, that is from likeness through mixtures of degrees of likeness and difference to complete difference. Soskice's way of dividing has the advantage of removing metaphor from literal analogy and highlighting its figurative nature. Indeed the very term "improper" analogy (which is what metaphor is) implies that it is not analogy at all. By definition it (metaphor) is an implicit comparison of one thing with something which is essentially other. The point or points of similarity are limited, there is a high degree of suggestion and a lot is left to the imagination. However I agree with Soskice that metaphor cannot be reduced to simile.

We might note that on both proposed divisions, both univocal and equivocal terms, considered not absolutely (for instance the proper sense given in a dictionary) but relatively (that is to other uses of the terms) may be either literal or metaphorical.[5]

Metaphor has been defined tentatively by Soskice, a linguistic philosopher, as: " ... that figure of speech whereby we speak about one thing in terms which are seen to be suggestive of another".[6] The *Macquarie Dictionary* defines it as "a figure of speech in which a term or phrase is applied to something to which it is not literally applicable, in order to suggest a resemblance, as 'A mighty fortress is our God' ". Allegory is a prolonged metaphor. The same dictionary defines it as "figurative treatment of one subject under the guise of another; a presentation of an abstract or spiritual meaning under concrete or material forms".

We should note too the possible use of other terminology in this discussion. The late Dr Thomas Muldoon used the distinction of a "strict" sense as opposed to a "broad" sense when applying sacrifice to cultic actions and good works. The New Testament itself speaks of "spiritual" priesthood and sacrifice, I think as opposed to the customary literal ones. I understand both Muldoon's "broad" and the New Testament's "spiritual" as meaning "religious-metaphorical".

II

Turning to the assertion that Jesus is a priest, it should be clear that the mere fact that Jesus is called a priest in the New Testament does not necessarily mean that he is literally a priest. This statement may be metaphorical. After all, he is also called a lamb, a shepherd, a gate, a vine, a rock, a bridegroom, a cornerstone, a builder. Metaphor was one of the favorite literary devices of the Bible. God is called a rock, a fortress, he has eagle's wings. Jesus calls Simon the rock on which he will build his church, promises him keys, gives him the care of his sheep, tells him to bind and loose.

Most authors discussing the priesthood of Christ do not even consider the possibility of it being a figurative use of the term. According to the second way of dividing language noted above, the very first judgment that must be made about a statement is whether it is meant figuratively or literally. Making the wrong judgment at this initial stage is a blunder. To fail to make the judgment altogether (at least implicitly) is, for a professional theologian, gross dereliction. I could name half a dozen authors who have written complete treatises on priesthood and have not even considered the possibility that it is attributed to Christ typologically or metaphorically and this despite Smith's work, which they probably have not read. His work should not be ignored. If it is wrong it should be refuted. I believe it is right.

The crucifixion of Jesus was a scandal for many to whom the Gospel was first preached: as Paul wrote: " ... but we preach Christ crucified—a stumbling block to Jews, and an absurdity to Gentiles" (1 Corinthians 1:23). A literal historical description left it as the execution of one judged to be, albeit unjustly, a criminal. It needed a lot of explanation to bring out its salvific value. So it was soon described figuratively by a variety of images (as, for example victory, redemption, a juridical process) including sacrifice. In fact in the New Testament it is described as a Passover sacrifice, an atonement sacrifice (Hebrews), a peace-offering, a covenant sacrifice. But the first one to think of drawing out this description to the point of describing Jesus as a priest was the author of Hebrews. This is the only book in the New Testament which so describes him. In doing this the author was being brilliantly original. He had a poetic mind. He was using allegory, or extended typology, which fits into the category of metaphor. This is not to deny divine inspiration.

THE VALUE OF METAPHOR

Why do we use metaphor? Why does it work? Obviously we are making some sort of comparison as in literal analogy but we are making a bigger jump across categories. A good original metaphor causes surprise. Our imagination gets something of a shock and we are moved to admire, laugh, detest or whatever more strongly.

Metaphor has the power to grab our attention, to raise our spirits from the humdrum of the literal, to fire our imaginations, to lift up our hearts, to make us feel our worth as humans, as beings with hearts and minds, with intelligence and emotions, creatures only a little below angels. Metaphors point us in the direction of transcendence. They are the symbols of language. They adorn poetry and they are most apt tools for the expression of religious experience. Yet metaphor has it hazards.

The first and obvious risk in the use of metaphor, and some other tropes (for example hyperbole, synecdoche, anthropomorphism), is that it be taken literally. A gospel example of this is Jesus' warning about the leaven of the Pharisees which the disciples took literally (*Matthew* 16:6-12).

Secondly, there is the problem of dead metaphors. Metaphors can become dead when they are used so much they are taken literally. Frequently this is no great cause for alarm if the matter is of no practical consequence, as when we speak of the "foot" of a mountain. In the interpretation of Scripture, I suggest it is important to realize when an author is using metaphor. When such a metaphor, after much use, becomes "dead" we should not accept it as a new literalism, but revive its original meaning.

Another hazard of metaphor is that it be pushed too far. Even though it suggests a chain reaction of ideas we may be tempted to go beyond what the originator had in mind even to a point where it becomes absurd. The metaphor of redemption came from the practice of buying people back from slavery and giving them back their liberty. This is applied metaphorically to the work of Jesus on our behalf. The New Testament nowhere pushes it beyond that. For example, it does not ask or answer the question, to whom is the ransom price paid? However this question was asked eventually by some of the fathers: some suggested God the Father, some the devil. But they were wrong in asking the question. The metaphor was not meant to be taken that far. To suggest that the Father demanded such a price makes him seem to be an unloving Father and robs him of his initiative in bringing about our salvation. To suggest the devil implies that he had some power or claim over God. So, too, some of the parables of Jesus are at times pushed too far. Indeed the parables of the eleventh hour workers and the prodigal son were really finished once they had illustrated God's care for the poor and the sinner: only the human inquisitiveness about fairness to those who do not classify themselves with the subjects of the parables required further additions or explanations by preachers.

A related hazard is the attempt to put metaphors into syntheses. Obviously the metaphor of Jesus as a builder should not be put together with that of him as the keystone. I suggest too that the metaphors of Jesus as priest and the Christian community as a priestly people do not necessarily have to be synthesized, as they are not (synthesized) in the New Testament.

The most obvious drawback of metaphor, at least to the logical or scientific mind, is its lack of accuracy, in that it is always liable to misinterpretation. Hence literal language is preferred in scientific treatises, legal documents such as wills, constitutions, treaties or trade negotiations.

METAPHORS AND SYMBOLS

I define symbol here as an object or action, or combination of both which is in the category of sign. It is in the real world as distinct from the literary world of words—mental, written or spoken. A bare sign is fairly univocal, is often functional and its task and significance are soon exhausted. The green light says "go", we do and forget it. The symbol suggests a whole chain of ideas, it is more open-ended, it points beyond itself, it opens up ongoing possibilities.

A birthday cake not only suggests the ingredients that it contains. Nor does it only suggest human nourishment, even agreeable nourishment. It is a symbol of a person, of one who is cherished in her community, whose parents remember her conception and birth, childhood and maturation, who herself is grateful for the love received, who is conscious of growth and who looks forward to a future.

Ashes can conjure up nostalgic memories of happy hours spent around a campfire, of singing old songs with friends, barbecuing sausages on the end of a stick, sharing ghost stories, of golden moments forever gone. The ashes in the urn at Lord's cricket ground have inspired enough books to fill a library. The birthday cake and the ashes are symbols. So are the sacraments. They are not bare signs. The sacramental priest is a symbol of Christ the "priest".

I now suggest that the metaphor does in the literary arena what the symbol does in the real.[7] As a by-product I suggest too that the metaphor is related to the symbol as the simile is related to the bare sign. Just as the bare sign does not suggest a chain reaction of related ideas but usually only one, so too the simile suggests a comparison but soon "runs out of steam". True, a simile can be very effective and suggestive: "My love is like a red, red rose..." Nevertheless metaphor is even more suggestive and open-ended. Like the symbol it transcends itself. It takes language, clothes it like Cinderella, enhances its value, gives it new meaning.

The preacher who can use figurative language, especially metaphor, effectively, will experience the attention of his listeners and the satisfaction of feeling that he has communicated something of himself and his own experience.

The magic of metaphor has intrigued philosophers of language at least since the time of the ancient Greeks. Biblical authors reveled in it because they sensed it was the only available human way of speaking about God. It has a built-in and admitted inadequacy and points the way to the transcendent because God is essentially beyond our experience and our abilities of expression.

INTERPRETING REALITY

One author has said that part of the human condition is the necessity of interpreting reality. Science and metaphysics try to describe reality with the greatest possible objectivity. In certain circumstances this does not work because of the background of the people between whom communication is being attempted. When a pre-technological people come into contact for the first time with sophisticated modern technology, they sometimes resort to cargo-cult "explanations". Communicators will attempt to explain new ideas by reference to already-understood concepts. Explanations of difficult or supernatural realities present even greater challenges. Scientific or metaphysical concepts which try to give exact descriptions are of no use in many circumstances, as when the reality is too far removed from the experience of the learning subject or in the case of the supernatural when the reality is intrinsically beyond human experience. Recourse is then had to figurative language which has the characteristics described above, that is of suggesting directions rather than attempting comprehensive description.

A good example of this is provided in Fr Paul Glynn's book, *A Song for Nagasaki*. Following the atomic bombing of Nagasaki, a requiem mass was held in the remains of the Catholic cathedral over which the bomb exploded killing thousands, including the wife of Dr Ngai, who himself had previously been converted to Catholicism. Having already attained great public respect for his heroic efforts as an army doctor and as a radiographer and as one who was already suffering from cancer because of his pioneering work in that field, he was asked to speak. His explanation of the bombing of Nagasaki was imaginative and provocative. "Was not Nagasaki the chosen victim, the lamb without blemish, slain as a whole-burnt offering on an altar of sacrifice, atoning for the sins of all nations during World War II?" He described it as a "holocaust" in the cultic sense. As Fr Glynn narrates, some of the congregation were angered by the metaphor and shouted out their disapproval.[8]

INTERPRETING THE CRUCIFIXION

The first efforts of the disciples to explain the significance of the crucifixion of Jesus were to describe it as fulfillment of the Hebrew Scriptures, in terms for example of the suffering servant and other types and prophecies. To Gentile audiences Paul drew from backgrounds with which they were more familiar (law courts, war, temple worship and so on). I am asking: were not *all* these explanations figurative? Because the event hovers between the divine and the human, only language with implications of transcendence is appropriate. The death of the God-man is so unique that it can be described only by reference to something *other*. Because there is nothing else in its own species, the only descriptions are by reference to other species that may have some similarities, and that is what we call metaphor.

The *Letter to the Hebrews* is one of the church's favorite texts. It is used for example in the masses of Christmas Day, the Presentation, the Annunciation, Good Friday, Corpus Christi, and on the weekdays of the first four weeks of Ordinary time of Year A. It is read in the divine office of Passiontide.

Why is it such a favorite? It is poetic. It distracts us from the horror of the reality of Christ's death; it gives meaning to something so apparently tragic and senseless. The Catholic tradition has in general tried to balance the realism of Christ's death with the symbolism used to bring out its ultimate meaning. Whilst there are crucifixes of Christ the Priest (i.e., with the figure clothed in priestly garments) in some churches, most have a realistic crucifix on the main wall. This realism is, I think, neatly counterbalanced by the symbolism of the eucharist. The mass-sacrifice is the sacramental interpretation of the crucifixion as a "sacrifice", though in the common of the mass there is no explicit reference to Christ as priest.

How do you tell when language is metaphorical? How do you tell when it is literal? If everyone immediately, naturally and spontaneously uses a word of a certain reality, it is a sign that the description is literal. Jesus never called himself a priest. The apostles never called him a priest. Nor did any of the writers of New Testament books except one. The author of *Hebrews* had no impact on the other writers of the New Testament and some Christians were unsure of the book's inspiration for several centuries. It was an original contribution of this author who alone drew out the image of sacrifice (which originated with Jesus himself at the Last Supper) to the point of saying that Jesus was not only the "victim" but also the "priest" of "sacrifice". Later authors would describe him also as the "altar" and the "temple".

The full argument for the metaphorical nature of Christ's priesthood is developed by Jerome Smith in the study already referred to (see note 2, above). To call Jesus a priest may be a "dead" metaphor, that is to say that it may have been used so often and for so long that people have forgotten it is a metaphor and taken it as literal. But even a dead metaphor is a metaphor and if it is revived it may regain its vitality and force. I believe this is necessary too if we are to arrive at the true relationship between Calvary and the eucharist, between the "priesthood" of Christ and the sacramental priesthood.

Some people think that the description of Jesus' priesthood as being metaphorical diminishes its value. But this would be more true if we adopted the other options. If the right description is not figurative it must be literal. To put Jesus into the same species as Levitical priests is contrary to *Hebrews* and undermines his uniqueness. Can we claim that he is in a different species of the same genus, or, in other words that we are using proper analogy of proportionality? We saw above that generic and specific predication is not proportionality but what was sometimes described as analogy of inequality, which the tradition agreed was reducible to univocity or synonymity. We can indeed give the term "priest" a more generic meaning, such as mediator, but we are then getting away from the usual meaning of priesthood and we are still putting Jesus into a category with others, thereby destroying his uniqueness and transcendence. If we put him in a species of priesthood different from Levitical priests but within the same genus, so that the essence of priesthood is preserved in both his and their priesthood, even though his is on a higher level, we are still putting him within a category (even though it be a generic category) in which the essence of priesthood is shared by both analogates, that is, Jesus and other priests. The point of proper proportional analogy is that the characteristic being compared is found essentially in both terms. Some have tried to escape this conclusion by denying that other priesthoods are true, but that makes non-sense out of the way the human mind works. The function of metaphor is to indicate an open-ended comparison, it points in a direction without imposing limitations because the underlying assumption is that *a* is not *b*. Something is said about one thing as though it were another. So to assert something metaphor-ically is implicitly to deny it literally.

Jesus was so unique that no one pre-existing category could hold him. So, many images were used from different fields: he is the light, the way, the life, the truth, shepherd, the pioneer and so on. All of these are obviously metaphorical. Is it surprising then that a poetically-minded author should draw a metaphor from the area of cult, especially when a start had already been made with the use of the metaphor of sacrifice, for example in the writings of Paul? On the other hand, if the priesthood of Jesus had been literally true would it not have occurred to many from the very start? A sign of literal truth is that it naturally springs to everyone's mind as the primary description.

Some theologians, such as M Barth and L-M Chauvet, have explicitly asked the question: "Was the death of Jesus a sacri-fice?"[9] Barth's treatment is disappointing. Like other Protest-ants he seems reluctant to explore the possibility of a metaphorical usage. I think they realize that if this is admitted the Catholic church may be able to answer the related question of the sacrificial nature of the mass. Others have written comprehensive works on ministry, for instance the Catholic Bernard Cooke, without even considering the possibility that Jesus was called a priest metaphorically. Some have perceived that the death of Jesus is called sacrifice metaphorically, for example Bruce Vawter. As far as I know, only Jerome Smith (besides the present author) has written strenuously to propose that Jesus is a priest in a metaphorical sense.

The literal acceptance of Jesus' priesthood has forced theo-logians to an explanation of ordained ministers as being priests by participation in the unique priesthood of Christ whereas the correct understanding, in my opinion, is that they, literal priests, are thereby sacraments of Christ interpreted precisely as "priest". The literal interpretation has also made the "essen-tial" distinction between ordained priesthood and the general priesthood of Christians (asserted in the Second Vatican Council's *Constitution on the Church*, no. 10) difficult to define.

III
CHRISTIAN SACRAMENTS AS LITERAL

The ordained Christian priest (*sacerdos*) is literally a priest but by proper analogy with priests of the Old Testament. To put it another way we could let "priesthood" be a genus with pagan, Jewish and Christian priests being species. The specific note about Christian priests would be that they are explicitly sacraments of Christ, they essentially refer back to him, depend entirely for their existence on him, they represent him, they perform actions as his instruments, "without him they can do nothing". *They interpret Jesus as "priest"*. Paradoxically, to do this they must be literal priests.

To determine whether things are literally what they are called should be the easiest of exercises. All you have to do is look at them, see what they are and do, observe what everyone naturally calls them. Or you can define your word and see if it applies to that thing or person. If you define a priest as "one whose office it is to perform religious rites, and especially to make sacrificial offerings" (*Macquarie Dictionary*), you should have no difficulty agreeing that the Christian *sacerdos* is literally a priest. Protestants might think this was a wrong development, but they would agree that the argument involves a claim by Catholics and others about literal priesthood.

To further illustrate this point let us look at the other sacraments. (For more detail see my *Sacrifice and Symbol*, ch 2.)

Baptism is a literal washing with literal water symbolizing spiritual "cleansing". Confirmation is a literal anointing, again symbolizing spiritual consecration. In the eucharist we start with literal bread and wine. The symbolism of penance can be more appreciated from the ancient rite in which there was a literal and public separation and readmission. The sacrament of the sick involves again a literal application of ointment. Orders has a literal imposition of hands. Matrimony involves a literal man and woman, bridegroom and bride, to be the symbols of Christ and his church. What the sacrament is called, it is that literally. So the sacramental priest is a priest literally, and indeed must be if he is to be the symbol depicting Christ as priest. That is his essential sacramental sign value, where he essentially differs from the merely baptized. In the area of sacramentals you need a literal light to symbolize Christ the "light of the world".

Nevertheless we must admit that some metaphors come across into Christian ministry and remain metaphors in their human subjects, for example, the metaphor of "shepherd". Jesus described himself as the good shepherd, the apostles were given shepherd roles and modern ministers are still described as "pastors". This happens in other instances as well, take, for example, the metaphor of "head".

SIGNS OF THE LITERAL AND FIGURATIVE

Literal speech is that which describes by words used in their primary accepted meaning. It is that which comes naturally, that which is most commonly used in descriptions of a reality by different people at different times. It is the straight historical narrative. So the events at the end of the life of Jesus of Nazareth are usually described, both in the New Testament and afterwards as his passion and death.

Good figurative descriptions are original to a particular author. They will vary from author to author, a number of them may be used to describe the same reality. It is important that the figurative be recognized as such or momentous errors may result. This is particularly true in the case of metaphorical language.

In a study of this point with regard to the Bible, G B Caird spends eleven pages describing the principles for determining when an author intends his words to be taken non-literally, that is, figuratively. These can be summarized as: explicit statement, the impossibility of literality, low correspondence, high development, juxtaposition of images, and originality.[10]

In writing the above I have kept in mind the realities we are concerned with but I think they can be applied generally. If we work through the New Testament descriptions of the final events of the gospel story, we find historical narrative interspersed with theological explanation, usually by the use of metaphors taken from a variety of backgrounds. The gospels themselves have a fairly straight narration of the events with some interpretation by the seeing of the events as fulfillment of the Hebrew Scriptures, especially prophecy. But prescinding from these, the description is of what happened in ordinary human language, that is literal language. In the *Acts of the Apostles* this literal description continues. The earliest efforts to explain these events, in themselves a stumbling block to Jews and folly to Greeks, was in terms of fulfillment of Scripture. Nevertheless Peter soon has recourse to figurative speech. In his Pentecostal sermon he speaks of the resurrection as the vindication by God of an unjust killing. Later Paul describes the events in juridical terms (justification). He also sees them as the offering of our Passover. Other descriptions are in military terms, that is to say of victory over death. The metaphor of redemption envisages the background of the practice of buying someone back from slavery. The death and resurrection are described by Jesus and Paul as baptism, submersion and emersion. The work of going through the whole New Testament and tradition to find all the explanations of the Jesus event is, I think, still waiting to be done.

The description of Jesus' death as a sacrifice does not fit the signs of literal language but does fit those of metaphor. That is, it is not found everywhere, it is not the only description. It is one taken from the cultic sphere, just as others are taken from the military, the juridical, the commercial, the social. It originates probably from Jesus himself at the Last Supper, and it can be found in a number of texts in the New Testament. It was accepted so well that it became a "dead metaphor", that is, it was taken by many as a literal statement.

The signs of metaphor are even more obvious in the case of the description of Jesus as priest. It is the creation of only one New Testament writer, the author of *Hebrews*. The fact that earlier writers or speakers, including Jesus, did not push the metaphor of sacrifice to the point of asking who was the priest, is itself an indication of its figurative nature. Biblical figures, like others, had their limitations, and were obviously not intended to be filled out to the utmost degree of detail. Sometimes such extensions became awkward or even ridiculous, as we have seen in the case of the redemption metaphor. In this particular case (sacrifice to priesthood) it worked. From the metaphor of Jesus as the new Passover sacrifice there eventually came the concept of Jesus as not only the victim but also the priest. This happened in the literary sphere in *Hebrews* and in the sacramental sphere in the ordination of Christian priests. The latter was implicit in the eucharistic words and gestures of Jesus at the Last Supper and its explicitation is a good example of the development of doctrine. Moreover, in the liturgical sources which describe Jesus as a priest, the metaphorical nature of the language is evident. Thus, the preface for Easter V is headed, "Christ is priest and victim", and goes on to say " ... he showed himself to be the priest, the altar, and the lamb of sacrifice".

IV

At this point it may be asked whether it is possible to describe the ultimate meaning of Jesus and his salvific work in literal language alone, that is, without recourse to metaphor. Clearly, it is not possible to discourse about God without the use of analogy. Certainly it has been said that what we can say about God is more untrue than true. It may be further asked whether we can appropriately use only improper analogy, or metaphor, when speaking of God. To safeguard his transcendence it could be argued that this is the case as God is completely "other" in comparison with anything we know or can imagine. Is this still the case when we come to the incarnation? The Word was made flesh and dwelt amongst us, the Word was expressed in human terms. The mystery once hidden is revealed. But can the mystery of Christ be expressed in literal human language?

St Paul, speaking about the crucifixion, would suggest not. In *1 Corinthians* 1:17 he writes: "Christ sent me to preach the good news, but not in the terms of philosophy in which the crucifixion of Christ cannot be expressed." I infer from this that the mystery of Christ, the mystery of grace won for us by his suffering and death, cannot be adequately expressed in the terms of philosophy, science, or any form of literal language, including properly analogical. Nor can it adequately be expressed in figures of speech, but as I have said, these disclaim adequate expression by their very definition. So we use a number of figures of speech, a variety of metaphors, and admit that the reality excels even their sum.

The difficulty of getting to a literal description is borne out in a recent article in the Adventist journal *Ministry*, entitled "Pauline Images of Salvation". The author lists justification-righteousness, redemption, reconciliation, salvation, imputation, honor, grace, "through Christ, in Christ, by Christ", sanctification, atonement, and victory. His fourth example is salvation, the word in the title of his article. So salvation is an image of salvation! I could quote similar examples in Catholic authors. It seems to suggest that all the words we use to describe what Jesus did are images, that is, figures of speech, metaphors.

The contemporary church is faced with the need for more relevant language in its proclamation of the meaning of Christ. This is perhaps best done in terms of his absolute commitment to the mission entrusted to him by the Father.

THE CHRISTIAN COMMUNITY AS PRIESTLY

The community addressed in *1 Peter* is lauded with epithets royal and priestly: "You, however, are 'a chosen race, a royal priesthood, a holy nation . . . '"(*1 Peter* 2:9; see also v 5). The author is quoting *Exodus* (19:6) where Israel was described as "a kingdom of priests". The same thought is also found in the *Apocalypse*. I do not think anyone interprets such sacerdotal phrases literally. Just as in Israel the *Exodus* text did not take away the prerogatives of the tribe of Levi, and did not attempt to imply that all were literally priests, so the metaphor is reapplied in the Christian era to bring out the necessity of sincere concern for the things of God, the need to offer him the spiritual sacrifices of holy lives, which was the essence of Christ's own "sacrifice".

So the "priesthood" of the baptized is metaphorical. It was rightly emphasized as an important metaphor by the Second Vatican Council while at the same time its "essential" difference from ordained priesthood was insisted upon. The nature of this essential difference was spelt out in *Presbyterorum ordinis*, n. 2: "Through that sacrament [Orders] priests by the anointing of the Holy Spirit are signed with a special character and so are configured to Christ the priest in such a way that they are able to act in the person of Christ the head." Here there is use of two metaphors, that of cult and that of the body. I am suggesting that the essential difference may also be expressed: the "priesthood" of the baptized (in relation to the usual dictionary concept of priesthood) is metaphorical, while that of the ordained is literal. The "offering" of the general priesthood is that of a holy life, whilst that of the ordained priest is in the visible order and is the gifts of bread and wine to be consecrated into the body and blood of Christ, symbols of his spiritual "offering" of himself in loving obedience to the Father.

SHOULD WOMEN WANT TO BE PRIESTS?

One of the fathers has a surprising comparison of the ranks of the Christian hierarchy: he compares the bishop with God the Father, the presbyterate with the apostles and the deacon with Jesus! Certainly Jesus nowhere calls himself a priest but he did cast himself in the role of servant and taught his disciples to adopt that role themselves. Christian holiness is to be found in the imitation of Christ particularly according to this model. If it is pointed out that Jesus was not a priest literally, it will help us to keep the role of the Christian priest in the right perspective when looking at the whole spectrum of Christian life. Nobody and no one role in the mystical body reflects the whole reality of Jesus: even the totality is defective. But the vocation of every individual is a witness to some aspect of that inexhaustible richness of the mystery of Christ. The Christian priest, *sacerdos*, plays out one role interpreting the willingness of Christ to give his life in loving obedience to the Father's plan. The model happens to be taken from the divinely-instituted liturgy of the people of God in its stage before Christ when priests were in fact male only. Whether the reasons for this were merely sociological or there were deeper anthropological or philosophical ones is beyond the scope of this chapter.

That women may not aspire to this *sacerdotal* role should not therefore be a matter of great concern. A male cannot be the sacrament of Christ's bride, the church, within the symbolism of marriage. If we distinguish other aspects of Christian ministry in the actual concrete existence of bishops and presbyters, such as their administrative and pastoral roles, their teaching or preaching duties, we may be in a different debate. In fact women are already performing many of these activities. It may be possible to give greater jurisdictional authority to women than is given at the moment. This is a subject wider than the present essay allows. The question of women in the priesthood is taken up in chapter 7 of this volume.

[1]Brian Francis Byron, *Sacrifice and Symbol—A New Theology of the Eucharist for Catholic and Ecumenical Consideration*, Catholic Institute, Sydney, 1991

[2]Jerome Smith, *A Priest Forever: A Study of Typology and Eschatology in the Epistle to the Hebrews*, Sheed and Ward, London, 1969

[3]Wim A De Pater, *Analogy, Disclosures, and Narrative Theology*. An extended version of two essays for *Handbuch Sprächphilosophie/Handbook Philosophy of Language*, ed. K Lorenz et al., De Gruyter, Berlin 1989, translated from the German by David K Wilken, pro manuscripto 1988, 5–6.

[4]J F Ross, in *Portraying Analogy*, Cambridge University Press, Cambridge 1981, 114–5, argues (against Cajetan) that metaphors need not be literally false. I can see that this may be true of negative statements (e.g., "He is not a footballer's bootlace").

[5]De Pater, op. cit., 11. A term used metaphorically of two different subjects (in comparison to its literal use of a third subject) is used univocally relative to these two cases: *foot*/mountain, *foot*/hill, cf. human foot.

[6]Janet Martin Soskice, *Metaphor and Religious Language*, Clarendon Press, Oxford 1985, reprinted 1988

[7]Since finishing *Sacrifice and Symbol*, I have been speculating further along these lines of paralleling figures of speech with types of sign: so besides comparing similes with bare signs and metaphors with symbols, I have concluded that synecdoche parallels the "symbolic reality" I use in my theology of the "real presence" of Christ in the eucharist (*Sacrifice and Symbol* ch. 10). The semitic synecdoche is particularly appropriate for this purpose because it uses not so much a part for a whole but an element for the whole, as for example *seed* for posterity, *flesh and bone*, or *flesh and blood*, for humanity or a section of it. In such contexts the terms transcend the physiological whilst still encompassing it.

[8]Paul Glynn, *A Song for Nagasaki*, The Catholic Book Club, Hunters Hill, NSW, 1988, 117–8

[9]M Barth, "Was Christ's Death a Sacrifice?", *Scottish Journal of Theology*, Occasional Papers no. 9, Oliver and Boyd, Edinburgh and London. 1961. L-M Chauvet, *Symbole et sacrement. Une relecture sacramentelle de l'existence chrétienne*, Les Editions du Cerf, Paris, 1988, ch. 8, II, 2, asks whether the life and death of Jesus was a sacrifice.

[10]G B Caird, *The Language and Imagery of the Bible*, Duckworth, London, 1980, 186–97

FIVE

The Giving of the Priesthood to the Faithful

David Orr

Our generation has seen a great interest shown in the theme of the priesthood of the faithful. The Second Vatican Council could speak strongly of the faithful sharing in the unique priesthood of Christ. It is important to note that this affirmation was made in the context of a reforming Council which had established liturgy as its primary document. Significantly, liturgy is at the heart of the exercise of the priesthood given the faithful. However, today, thirty years after the beginning of the Council, there seems to be little interest in preaching or celebrating the priesthood of all Christians. The topics of liturgy and priesthood seem to have agenda other than their interrelatedness.

To better establish and understand the relationship between the priesthood of the faithful and the liturgy, this chapter will study the interrelatedness of these themes, and their interrelatedness in the patristic and liturgical traditions of our Roman church. We will then survey the way recent theological opinion on the giving of the priesthood to the faithful has attempted in this century to unite these themes. Finally it will be of importance to reflect upon the pastoral significance of the theme of the priesthood of the faithful based upon the liturgical experience of the past thirty years.

EVIDENCE FROM THE PATRISTIC TRADITION

Some of the fathers of the Roman church are consistent in claiming the gift of the Spirit as the source of the priesthood given the faithful. As Leo expresses it so strongly: "the anointing of the Spirit consecrates priests".[1] His reason is that the Spirit was the source of consecration of Christ himself, in whom the Christian is inserted by initiation. Christ was empowered at his baptism to embark upon his life of obedience to the Father and so render acceptable worship to the Father. So, too, the Christian is empowered by the gift of the Spirit to offer that same sacrifice to the Father—to be the human element by which Christ exercises his priesthood today.

The patristic tradition is clear that this *gift* of the Spirit is distinguished from the *action* of the Spirit. Tertullian reflects this well when he speaks of the Spirit working in the waters of baptism, but being given in the imposition of hands.[2] It is common for the Roman patristic tradition to make such a distinction—they saw the two moments of baptism in water and imposition of hands as two distinct actions in the one ritual of Christian initiation.

The giving of the Spirit to the newly-baptized was identified with the imposition of hands—an imposition usually reserved to the ministry of the bishop. This ritual finds its justification in the apostolic church's act of imposing hands for the giving of the Spirit—the fathers can call upon diverse texts of the New Testament to justify this association.

Importantly, this giving of the Spirit was spoken of by the priestly term of an "anointing" of the person. This terminology finds its justification in the language of the New Testament. The synoptics had presented the event of Jesus' baptism in the Jordan as an "anointing" by the Spirit. This language was to color the patristic understanding of this event.[3] Significantly in early Christian art, the baptism of Jesus was associated with John the Baptist imposing hands upon Jesus, rather than pouring water;[4] presumably because the central element of this event was the giving of the Spirit—a giving the church was to link with the imposition of hands. However, this giving was spoken of in terms of an anointing of the person to link the celebration with the event of Jesus' own life, and so be able to draw upon the rich tradition of the Old Testament, which spoke of the anointing of priests. Initially, then, the giving of the priesthood to the faithful was linked with this anointing by the Spirit.[5]

Having begun to speak of this giving of the Spirit in terms of anointing, it was always possible for this spiritual anointing (that is anointing by the Spirit) to find expression in a physical anointing. It was not uncommon in the Latin tradition to include an anointing with the imposition of hands. Hippolytus (writing around 219 AD) refers to an anointing of the person who had received the Spirit,[6] which did not prevent him from including an anointing with baptism in water;[7] he distinguishes these two anointings by a distinction of ministers—the first given by the presbyter, and the second by the bishop. Ambrose (+397 AD) would later speak of the post-baptismal presbyteral anointing as like the anointing of an athlete preparing for contest, and not in the biblical tradition of anointing of kings and priests.[8] Thus the liturgical tradition of the Roman church (besides a physical anointing following baptism in water) knew both the "anointing" by the giving of the Spirit in episcopal imposition of hands, and the physical anointing of the person (who had received the Spirit) with chrism.

Chrism, (a word which the fathers identified with "Christ"), was a valuable symbol in the liturgical celebration to explicate the gift of the priesthood to the faithful. It was easy for the fathers to draw upon the rich biblical tradition which linked anointing with the establishment of priesthood. However, the fathers were clear in claiming that the giving of the priesthood was not in the physical act of anointing, but in the anointing by the Spirit.[9] Difficulty arises with the Eastern liturgical tradition, which identified the giving of the Spirit with the anointing of the person with chrism. In the face of such a tradition, it was not uncommon for confusion to enter regarding the giving of the Spirit: was it by way of imposition or by anointing with chrism, and which anointing (the post-baptismal presbyteral anointing, or the episcopal anointing)? This confusion was to become acute in our Roman church during the Middle Ages.

It must also be noted that in the Roman church, legislation was consistently invoked to support the right of only the bishop to impose hands.[10] Because of the frequent unavailability of the bishop, episcopal imposition was often not celebrated at the time of baptism in water. With this growing fragmentation of the unified ritual of Christian initiation, difficulty arose regarding the later ritual of imposition of hands. Divorced from its context of initiation, this ritual began to take on its own significance. Already, in the days of Jerome (+419 AD), ridicule could be poured upon this ritual—even though Jerome would support the tradition of the Spirit being given by this imposition. Aligned with this questioning, was the Eastern tradition which would prevent such a situation from arising by delegating to the presbyter the right to fully celebrate the ritual of initiation, if the bishop was unavailable for the celebration. In the Western liturgical tradition, this implied that the presbyter could both baptize in water and impose hands for the giving of the Spirit. Legislation appeared early in the Roman church to restrict, and even to prohibit this practice. Thus in the Roman church, imposition of hands for the giving of the Spirit was limited to the ministry of the bishop.

However, following the example of the East, some Western churches, particularly Gaul, allowed the presbyter to baptize and anoint for the giving of the Spirit, thereby completing the ritual for Christian initiation. When this practice came upon the legislation of the Roman church, under Charlemagne's liturgical reform, it seems that the Gallican church retained its unified ritual of initiation (baptism in water, anointing for the Spirit and eucharist) and added to it the Roman practice of "episcopal imposition of hands". In such a context, it is not surprising that the episcopal imposition fell into disuse—with its significance being seriously questioned.

Such a situation was already reflected in the Pentecost homily, attributed to Faustus of Riez. Already the ritual of episcopal imposition is fragmented from Christian initiation and he begins to speak of the significance of the episcopal imposition in terms of preparing the person to face the trials of life. Thus appears his much quoted opinion:

> In baptism, we are reborn to life; after baptism we are confirmed to fight. In baptism, we are washed; after baptism, we are strengthened.[11]

Such an opinion is far removed from the priestly understanding of Christian initiation by the fathers.

With the restoration by Charlemagne of the Roman practice of episcopal imposition to the Gallican initiation ritual, it was not surprising that the giving of priesthood continued to be linked with the post-baptismal anointing, and not with the imposition. It is important to note that such a change occurred in the context of a church which viewed the post-baptismal anointing as a pneumatic event, and not in the context of the Roman church which knew it only as an explicative action related to baptism in water (as witnessed in Hippolytus).

However, it was not long after the reintroduction by Charlemagne of the episcopal imposition, that the distinction made earlier by Faustus bears fruit. Alcuin begins to speak of the post-baptismal anointing in terms of anointing of the Christian to the priesthood of Christ: "You are the royal, priestly race, offering yourselves to God as the holy and pleasing sacrifice".[12] He will, however, go on to speak of the imposition of hands by the bishop for the gift of the Spirit "so that strengthened by the Holy Spirit they may preach to others".[13] Thus he would see the Christian sharing in the priesthood of Christ by the post-baptismal anointing, and then see the Christian being set apart by the gift of the Spirit to preach to others. He does not directly claim the giving of the priesthood to be in terms of the gift of the Spirit—although his use of patristic terminology in this context could be read in that light.

Rabanus Maurus was to explicate this teaching of Alcuin by directly speaking of two givings of the Spirit to the Christian— although he tried to retain some element of the sacerdotal significance of the episcopal action by linking it also with priesthood.

> For the baptized is signed on the top of the head with chrism for priesthood; however he is signed on the forehead by the bishop. The first represents the descent of the Spirit consecrating him as the dwelling place of God, while in the second, the sevenfold grace of the same Holy Spirit comes to him with all the fulness of holiness , knowledge and virtue.[14]

He clearly can speak of two distinct givings of the Spirit, although he tries to invoke both givings of the Spirit when he speaks of priesthood. Significantly this teaching of the two givings of the Spirit was in the liturgical context of a church where the laity had no active involvement in the liturgical celebrations. The total action of celebrating eucharist had moved to the ordained ministers.

It will then be this mixed understanding of the giving of the priesthood which will also appear in the liturgical tradition of the Latin, Roman church—able to invoke both the Old Testament tradition of a physical anointing to priesthood in general and the new tradition of the Spirit anointing the person to the priesthood of Christ. However, our tradition (even if it was unclear regarding the liturgical expression of the giving of the Spirit) was clear in linking the giving of the priesthood to the faithful with the giving of the Spirit. Important lessons can be gained from a study of the liturgy's own understanding to the exercise of this priesthood.

EVIDENCE FROM THE LITURGICAL TRADITION

The earliest prayer tradition of the Roman church, the *Veronense* (a book collating various sources of mass texts made towards the end of the sixth century) could speak of the community in terms of *1 Peter* 2:9 as being a community of priests (No. 1130). In other formulae it would see all the community exercising this priestly dignity in the action of offering "spiritual sacrifice"— that is the self-offering of each member of the liturgical assembly was deemed to be salvifically important for all the community. Of course, such an importance could only find its explanation in the unique sacrifice of Christ, of which the self-offering of the community was seen to be its sacrament.

This understanding was to be taken and developed in the *Gelasian* (a book explicitly prepared to serve the liturgical need of the presider; although the present copy of this sacramentary was copied in 750 AD, it has been shown to include material which originated in the sixth century). It too was able to affirm the dignity of the community as a community of priests (Nos 589 and 480). Although it did not repeat the text of the *Veronense*, it did repeat its teaching. It also began to reflect the relationship between this dignity and the giving of the Spirit—a giving it knew to be linked with imposition of hands. It was also able to develop this theme by developing the theme of chrism in its liturgy of Holy Thursday. Here, chrism is presented clearly in terms of its relationship with priesthood. Again, this relationship is not made just in terms of a physical anointing but in the patristic terms of "the oil of anointing": a clear reference to the giving of the Spirit.

While the *Gelasian* can freely speak of the priestly dignity of all the community, it also begins to reflect the growing importance of the ministerial priest in the liturgical action of the community. Its prayers do include all the celebrating community in the action of offering sacrifice—an offering to be made by all as their self-offering; however the importance now being given to the buildings and the elements needed in such buildings, begins to impinge upon its understanding of worship. With an increasing importance being given to things material, it is possible that even the "spiritual sacrifice" of the community could be reduced to a material sacrifice—instead of the material offering being expressive of the sacrifice made by each in their self-offering.

The *Gregorian* traditions of the sacramentary (again Roman texts explicitly prepared for liturgical celebrations and collated in the eighth and ninth centuries) are less explicit in declaring the priestly dignity of the community. The *Gregorian* does not provide any new texts, beyond those already given by the *Veronense* and the *Gelasian*, which develop the priestly dignity of the community—in fact, it is the very absence of these texts from its formulae that is evident. Its initiation texts now begin to reflect the element of forgiveness of sins, rather than the creative work of the Spirit in forming the priestly community. Its initiation ritual is very rudimentary, providing few details of its celebration. Its texts also begin to reflect the isolation of the community from the action of eucharist—an isolation expressed both in ministries and architecture.

While the celebration of the giving of the Spirit by episcopal imposition is reflected throughout the sacramentary tradition, it is well known that its celebration in the Roman tradition began to be dramatically separated from baptism in water because of the growing absence of the bishop from the celebration of Christian initiation. Thus there began to develop a separate celebration around the distinct celebration of episcopal imposition. This tradition makes its appearance in the pontificals of the Roman church.

The pontificals reflect the growing importance of this ritual as being the preserve of the bishop. The Roman church had always retained its celebration as an episcopal celebration, but had allowed the presbyter to minister it on occasions. In the pontificals this exception disappears, and only the bishop appears as its minister. The theological issues which were discussed previously begin to impinge upon this liturgical practice. This is formalized in the pontifical of William of Durand in the thirteenth century where the episcopal imposition has developed its own ritual, independent of Christian initiation, and now set in the context of parish visitation by the bishop; included in this ritual is a novel expression of the sign of peace, a slap on the cheek.

The pontifical sermon which began to accompany the consecration of chrism on Holy Thursday takes up much of the contemporary theology regarding this ritual: it still views the giving of the Spirit in terms of an imposition (although the pontifical of Durand will give much greater importance to the anointing), but begins to speak of an earlier giving of the Spirit by baptism in water. In fact the celebration of imposition is diminished in a context where it is taught that its celebration is no longer necessary for salvation (as expressed by the Scholastics).[15]

Consequently, episcopal imposition gives way in importance to the ritual of anointing, although the Roman tradition continues to retain the imposition—at one stage, the anointing itself is seen to be an imposition. The confusion regarding the giving of the Spirit will continue to inform the discussion of the significance of episcopal imposition. Recourse will be made to the teaching of Faustus to explain its significance in terms of it "perfecting" baptism. Anointing to priesthood will begin to appear in terms of the post-baptismal anointing. It is not surprising that once the priesthood is no longer linked with the giving of the Spirit, but with a physical anointing, in the liturgical reform of Pius V, the teaching of the priesthood of the faithful finds very little affirmation and even less liturgical expression in the life of the Roman church. The theme of the community sharing in the priesthood of Christ was not able to be affirmed in a context where the ministerial priesthood was under attack. The actual form of eucharistic celebration, in which the community has very little part (other than being listeners), did not encourage debate about the priestly role of the community in the action of eucharist.

The liturgical reform of this century has again returned the theme of the priestly action of the community to the discussion of liturgy. The reform of the liturgical texts of the Roman church by the Second Vatican Council has brought a constant proclamation of the priestly dignity of the community in the liturgical celebration.

> Through his cross and resurrection he freed us from sin and death and called us to the glory that has made us a chosen race, a royal priesthood, a holy nation, a people set apart.[16]

This recognition of the priestly dignity of all the community has accompanied an increasing participation by the faithful in the liturgy and has given rise to their experiencing their dignity in the very liturgical action.

However, this liturgical reform has not moved the discussion on the source of this priesthood beyond the teachings of the Carolingian period. A study of the reformed, liturgical texts shows the continuing confusion regarding the role of the Spirit in the formation of the community as a priesthood. The new texts will continually speak of the priestly dignity of the community and relate it to the waters of baptism—with the post-baptismal anointing with chrism as the expression of this dignity. After an infant's baptism in water, the presbyter prays, as he anoints the child: "as Christ was anointed priest, prophet and king, so may you live as a member of his body sharing everlasting life", without any reference to the gift of the Spirit. However other rituals will continue to speak of the giving of the Spirit by the episcopal imposition and anointing in the later celebration of confirmation. Clearly, the intimate relationship of the giving of the Spirit with the empowerment of the person to priesthood has been lost.

Again there is continuing imprecision regarding the giving of the Spirit; but the faithful are clearly called to exercise the priesthood given them by the Spirit and they are to exercise it by their offering of "spiritual sacrifices". The acceptance of the tradition of the Latin Roman church (which linked the gift of the Spirit with the faithful's empowerment to priesthood) is probably the best context for the contemporary church's effort to implement the call of the Second Vatican Council for the restoration of the full, active and conscious participation of the community in liturgy. It provides a firm basis for grounding the liturgical participation of God's people in their exercise of the priesthood of Christ: "We are called a holy people, a royal priesthood, a people set apart and a holy nation through your Son, our Lord Jesus Christ".[17] How has this call by the Vatican Council found expression in our generation? To answer this question, it is necessary to summarize the contemporary discussion on the priesthood of the faithful.

CONTEMPORARY THEOLOGICAL STUDIES

Building upon the biblical and patristic studies that have been taking place during this century, various theological reflections upon this theme have developed. As the biblical research began to accept the understanding of "basileon hiereutoma" of 1 *Peter* 2:9 as being the "royal priesthood", it was possible to turn attention to the exercise of this priesthood in the offering of the "spiritual sacrifice".[18] Again the question being raised here is that of the content of the "spiritual sacrifice": how an author views the Christian's sharing in the priesthood, determines how the author views the "spiritual sacrifice".

Botte distinguishes three possible understandings of priesthood which reflect three understandings of "spiritual sacrifice": firstly, it is purely a metaphorical priesthood (which would involve no real sacrifice as such); secondly, a mystical priesthood (established by union with Christ the priest and would entail the offering of the sacrifice of another, that is, of Christ); and thirdly a cultic priesthood (which may be related to an aspect of the ritual of Christian initiation, but which, for Botte, does not involve a real priestly power, as would be expressed in eucharist).[19] With regard to this third form, the conclusion of Cerfaux must also be included: "The priestly power of the faithful is always seen as metaphorical, never is it related to the celebration of eucharist.".[20] It is not certain that his use of the term "metaphorical" is the same as that of Botte, but it does reflect the thinking of Botte regarding the exercise of the priesthood of the faithful. Clearly, these authors see no direct connection between the "royal priesthood" and the eucharist. Even though the eucharist may be the bread of Christian living, the content of the eucharistic celebration is not seen to be included in the offering by the individual Christian.

This would seem to be the opinion of *Mediator Dei* when it speaks of Christians by baptism sharing the priesthood of Christ, but not enjoying any priestly function.[21] Christians "offer" the sacrifice by means of and in union with the hierarchical priest—an action the document calls "oblation", but not "immolation":[22] this the community achieves by sharing in the ritual (that is, by following silently what the hierarchical priest is doing) and by taking to themselves the moral attitude of Christ.[23] This highlights the fact that the people's part is a non-essential part—and so it can be claimed that the faithful have no part in the action.[24]

Congar in some of his writings would seem to accept this thought also.[25] However elsewhere he claims, "by baptism (and confirmation) every believer is set aside as celebrant of the mystery of Christ, and especially of the eucharist, where they are united to it and nourished by it".[26] This question of the relationship of the priesthood of the faithful to the eucharist seems to be crucial to the understanding of the exercise of the priesthood.

Most authors can accept the relationship between the priesthood of the faithful and the offering of "spiritual sacrifice"—a relationship already established in *1 Peter* 2:5. For many, this relationship is valid only when the "spiritual sacrifice" is a reference to the Christian living of the person—again Congar could be counted among such authors when he sees the "spiritual sacrifice" as "the spiritual worship that the offering of a good life is", an offering which cannot be properly defined in liturgical terms.[27] Others will go even further and link the self-offering of the Christian with that of Christ in the eucharist: "the eucharist is then for each of the baptized the external sign of their own personal offering united to that of Christ", is Lécuyer's understanding.[28] Here the relationship between Christian living and the eucharist is made, but the relationship is left in the realm of the symbolic: the interior offering made by the Christian is reflected in and even nourished by the celebration of eucharist; but can it be said that this relationship is more than just symbolic? Can it be claimed that the Christian's offering which is made by each Christian is the sacrament of the offering of Christ in the eucharist and so acceptable to the Father?

Certainly during this century this constitutive relationship between the Christian's offering and that of Christ has been claimed. Thils would advocate this "cultic power" by invoking the Thomistic understanding of the "sacramental character".[29] In a more recent work this relationship with the eucharist is explicated: "Christians ought to be aware of their capacity, their power of uniting themselves to the unique and perpetual sacrifice of their Head, by virtue of their baptism".[30] Feuillet will speak clearly of this relationship in terms of "oblation": "All the baptized, without distinction, take an active part in the eucharistic oblation which makes possible their own oblation".[31]

However, it will be the exegetical work of Vanhoye that lays a firm foundation for the "spiritual sacrifice" to be grounded in the eucharistic celebration by his analysis of *Hebrews* and *First Peter*.[32] He begins by distinguishing "spiritual sacrifice" from the carnal offerings made in the temple of the old law and from the mental offering familiar in philosophical thought.[33] He defines "spiritual sacrifice" in terms of "an offering made under the action of the Holy Spirit", quoting both *Romans* 15:16 and *Hebrews* 9:14.[34] Although this offering is made under the action of the Spirit, the offering itself is incarnational, rooted in the life of the Christian: "In reality, from the Christian point of view, true sacrifices are existential sacrifices: they consist in the transformation of existence by the action of the Holy Spirit, in union with the sacrifice of Christ".[35] The author wishes to emphasize the human dimension of such offerings; they do have a dimension which is temporal (in space and time), but their inspiration is grounded in the Holy Spirit.

Vanhoye can then discount the dilemma raised earlier by Elliot, who approaches 1 *Peter* 2:9 as being only a reference to the ministry of witness without reference to eucharist.[36] For Vanhoye, the dilemma does not exist if there is a correct understanding of "spiritual sacrifice":

If one were to retain only the Old Testament perspective, one would be unable to discover any direct link between these two aspects of the life of believers (i.e. witness and eucharist): in the Old Testament witness before the world did not form part of the priestly functions. But if one takes the Christian point of view, according to which true sacrificial worship consists in transforming human existence by means of the love which comes from God, one can then— and indeed one must—include in the "spiritual sacrifices" the activity of witness. This activity, in fact, forms an integral part in a life of love.[37]

Thus the full understanding of "spiritual sacrifice" is to be placed in the themes of witness *and* cult—for the Christian such cult is only possible by union with the one sacrifice of Christ.

The driving force which moves the Christian to existential sacrifice comes from the sacrifice of Christ, made present in the eucharist, and the fulfillment of existential sacrifices—their reaching God—is only possible through the mediation of the sacrifice of Christ, itself also made present in the eucharist. The latter then is clearly indispensable for existential sacrifice.

Building upon such a strong statement of the existential nature of the "spiritual sacrifice", Vagaggini will be able to express this exercise of "spiritual sacrifice" in terms of the faithful celebrating the sacrifice of the mass.[38]

This language, which refers to the Christian "as celebrating eucharist",[39] now brings us to an important issue which has molded the discussion of the theme of the priesthood of the faithful during this century: the question of the distinction between the priesthood of the faithful and that of the ministers. Luther had employed the theme of priesthood of the faithful to deny the role of the ministerial priest.[40] Throughout this century, Catholic writers have always been careful to avoid an equation of the ministry of the hierarchical priesthood and that of the laity. Lumen Gentium, being the first conciliar document to actually invoke the phrase "sacerdotium commune fidelium",[41] was to be strong in its affirmation that the two differ "not only in degree but also in kind".[42] In this way, the Second Vatican Council spoke both of the unity and the diversity of the ministry of the hierarchical priesthood and that of the laity: in fact the hierarchical priesthood is seen to be at the service of the priesthood of the laity and in fact presupposes the priesthood of the faithful.[43] However the Council, when speaking of the role of the laity in the eucharist will tend to employ the verb "exercere" to describe their role, rather than verbs like "celebrare".[44]

One of the developments in theological reflection which has aided the development of the understanding of the active role of the priesthood of the laity has been the development of a liturgical theology, which has given a new context to the discussion. The work of Casel provides an understanding of the liturgy as being the celebration of the mystery of Christ (and not just an external ritual)—in fact the liturgy is the realization of the one mystery of salvation, Christ, by the entire church.[45] This is further explicated in the work of Marsili who clearly spoke of Christian ritual as being the presence of the mystery of Christ in the church.[46] The important symbol here is that of the church itself—certainly the church as the body of Christ can be invoked as the cultic agent but is the individual member of the church also seen as a cultic agent?

Marsili was to begin by distinguishing the presence of Christ and the presence of the sacrifice of Christ—for him, Christ was present in the eucharist so that the church could share in the sacrifice of Christ; the whole church was called to share in that sacrificial act, and not just to render homage to Jesus present.[47] He developed this theme to remind the laity that their communion in the sacrifice of Christ (which is only possible by communion with gifts consecrated in that celebration)[48] was essential to their power to sacrifice (as distinct from sharing in the sacrificed Christ).[49] It is to this offering of the sacrifice of Christ that all Christians are primarily called in the action of eucharist—an action realized in the communion of that eucharist, expressing the Christian's willingness to live the sacrifice of Christ in his own life of self-giving. In communion, the Christian incarnates the sacrifice of Christ—for in the self-offering being made by the Christian (a human action), Christ's self-offering is rendered present in human history. Thus communion in the eucharist can never be reduced to a material action of eating and drinking, but must always be seen in the context of the mystery of Christ present in the sign of this sacramental ritual, the human action of eating and drinking, expressive of the self-offering of the individual, is the sacramental sign for the presence of the sacrifice of Christ.[50]

This ability of the Christian to share so intimately in the sacrifice of Christ (that is, to be the sacramental sign of this sacrifice) is founded, for Marsili, in Christian initiation, where the person is united with Christ. Empowered by the Spirit, the Christian is one with Christ. For Marsili this is not an analogous union of the person with Christ, but must be a real union; otherwise the sacrifice would not be the sacrifice of the entire church, here and now gathered as the body of Christ, head and members. So the Christian's sharing in the priesthood of Christ has to be a real sharing in priesthood.[51] This priesthood takes on concrete expression in the eucharist, where the Christian who lives a life of self-giving, modeled on that of Christ, provides the human context in time and space for the sacrifice of Christ to take form: "The spiritual sacrifice made by Christians in the holiness of living is the very material by which Christ is present, carrying to the perfection of the Head, the sacrifice of his Body which is the church".[52] The laity therefore not only render worship to Christ who is present in the eucharist; nor do they just offer Christ the victim, but in fact they incarnate the sacrifice of Christ in time and space by the very act of their own self-offering, which is the "very material" of that very sacrifice. It is this giving of one's life, (the sacrifice of the body of Christ, the church), which realizes the sacrifice of Christ the head.

Thus the Second Vatican Council was to speak of the liturgy as being the action of the whole church[53] and as being the exercise of the priesthood of Christ,[54] in which the baptized are to be actively involved;[55] this participation is seen as being demanded by the very nature of liturgy itself;[56] it is both the right and the duty of all the baptized to take their part in liturgy, particularly in the eucharist.[57] Building upon the need to express fully the Christian's being the sacrifice of Christ, the Council embarked upon the reform of the ritual of liturgy.[58] Yet how successful has been this reform?

THE SIGNIFICANCE OF THE THEME TODAY

History clearly shows that when the community was not involved actively in their celebration of liturgy, then the awareness of the priestly dignity of the community was lost. Once the community lost its ability to exercise its priesthood in the liturgical celebration, then their dependence upon an intermediary priesthood became apparent. The ministerial priest began to offer sacrifice for "them", instead of his leading them to make their own self-offering as the sacrament of Christ's once-and-for-all sacrifice.

The contemporary generation has tried to restore to the church the rich tradition of the full participation of all members in the celebration of liturgy. Soon after the Second Vatican Council, this led to a more active celebration which was not necessarily a deeper participation—people seemed to be attached to doing things in liturgy without knowing exactly why. As this novelty wore off, people drifted away from involvement. However, the basis for their previous involvement may have been inadequate.

The theme of the priesthood of the faithful provides a firm basis on which to build participation. The community does not get involved in liturgy just to do something; rather their action in liturgy must be the expression of their relationship with their Lord—even the important action of silence by a community must be expressive of the reflective stance of all the community (and not just of a patient marking of time). Without the constitutive contribution of all the community, the action is hollow. This contribution is termed in our liturgical tradition as being the "offering of spiritual sacrifice"—an offering which must extend beyond its religious expression in ritual to encompass the total fabric of Christian living so that the seamless garment of Christ's body (of prayer and living) may be credible. The community must be called to make their constitutive contribution to the building of eucharist—they are not just to be doing something at eucharist, but establishing eucharist. As

Benedict wrote in his rule for monks: when praying, their spirit must be in tune with their body.

Yet is it still useful today to speak of the *priesthood* of the faithful in a generation in which "priesthood" is so strongly identified with its ministerial expression? While the rejection of the term "priest" for the faithful may ease the burden of those advocating the essential differences between the ministerial priesthood and the priesthood of the faithful, it does not do justice to the church's invitation to acknowledge their inter-relatedness. The early patristic church would separate the two by speaking of all Christians being priests (*sacerdos*), while addressing her ministers as presbyters (*presbyter*). As the community began to lose its role in liturgy, it became common to term the ministers as priests (*sacerdos*). Today, as the community once again lays claim to its rightful place in liturgy, there is need to ground this process in the rich tradition of the church: it would seem that tradition invites us to rediscover the merit of knowing all Christians as priests and of recognizing the servant nature of those who are called to minister to this priestly community. Already we speak of bishops and deacons as signifi-cant terms for such ministers—maybe there is value also in highlighting the role of presbyters in their contribution of service to the priestly people of God. Such designation of the ministers would preserve the unity of the priesthood of Christ and enhance the dignity of the community, reminding the community of their vital contribution to the building of that body of Christ today. However, such solutions of language need to be grounded in the experiences of the celebrating commun-ity—the total community needs to recognize and respond to the invitation to exercise its priesthood. This invitation is not one to honor and power, but to conversion and holiness.

---

[1]*Tractatus iv*: 1 "Item alius in natale eiusdem", *CCL* 138:16

[2]"Dehinc manus inponitur per benedictionem aduocans et inuitans spiritum sanctum". *De Baptismo*. viii: *CCL* 1:283

[3]"Christus enim a chrismate, id est ab unctione, nomen accepit, iuxta quod dicitur: 'Unxit te deus, deus tuus, oleo laetitae', id est spiritu sancto". Bede, *Expositio Actuum Apostolorum*, iv: 27, *CCL* 121:27

[4]L De Bruyne, "L'imposition des mains dans l'art Chrétien ancien" in *Rivista de Archeologia Cristiana*, XX, 1943, 113–266

[5]"Christi autem sunt, qui Spiritu sancto unguntur". Jerome, *Tractatus de Psalmo CIIII, CCL* 78:190

[6]*Traditio Apostolica*. ch. 21: "De iis qui accipient baptismum". *La tradition apostolique de saint Hippolyte*. ed. B Botte, Münster, 1972, 52

[7]*La tradition apostolique de saint Hippolyte*. ed. B Botte, Münster, 1972, 50

[8]Ambrose, *De Sacramentis*. i:4 *SC* 25bis:62

[9]"Et quia est unctio spiritalis et nequaquam humani corporis, ut in sacerdotibus Iudaeorum". Jerome, *Commentariorum in Esaiam*. XVII, lxi:1–3, *CCL* 73a:706

[10]Cf. The much-quoted direction of Pope Innocent I: "Epistola ad Decentio", R Cabié, *La Lettre du Pape Innocent Ier à Decentius de Gubbio*, Louvain, 1973

[11]Faustus of Riez, "Homilia de Pentecosten", L Van Buchem, *L'Homélie Pseudo-Eucébienne de Pentcôte*, Nijmegen, 1967, 41

[12]Alcuin, Epistolae 134. "Alcvinus Oduino presbytero baptismi caeremonias exponit", *Momumenta Germaniae Historica: Epistolae Karolini Aevi*, Bk II, ed. E Duemmler, Berlin, 1895, 203

[13]Ibid.

[14]Rabanus Maurus, *De Clericorum Institutione*. Bk I:XXX, "De impositione manus episcopalis", *PL* 107:314A–B

[15]*S Th*. 3a q.65 a.4 Reply

[16]Preface of Sundays in Ordinary Time 1

[17]Ve 1130

[18]Although in *1 Peter* 2:5 this expression appears in the plural. Marsili notes that today its intent is better conveyed by the use of the singular. S Marsili, "La liturgia, momento storico della salvezza", *Anàmnesis*, Vol. I, Roma, 1974, 130

[19]"L'idée du sacerdoce des fidèles dans la tradition", *Cours et conférences des semaines liturgiques*, XI, Louvain, 1933, 24–25

[20]"Regale Sacerdotium", *Revue des sciences philosophiques et théologiques*, 28, 1939, 37

[21]"Nullo modo iure sacerdotali frui posse", *Mediator Dei*, AAS Vol. XXXIX, 1947, 554

[22]Ibid. 555

[23]"At cum potissimum christifideles liturgicae actioni tam pia intentaque mente coniunguntur, . . . vehementerque cupientes Iesu Christo", ibid. 558

[24]Ibid., 557

[25]"No ancient text . . . supports a transference of the worship and priesthood of the faithful from the place of Christian life to that of liturgical celebration", *Lay people in the Church*, Westminster, 1965, 136

[26]"Structure du sacerdoce chrétien", *La Maison Dieu*, 27, 1951, 71–2

[27]*Lay people in the Church*, Westminster, 1965, 137 and 136

[28]J Lécuyer, "Essais sur le sacerdoce des fidèles chez les Péres", *La Maison Dieu*, 27, 1951, 15

[29]"Le pouvoir cultuel du baptisé", *Ephemerides Theologicae Lovaniensis*, XV, 1938, 683–9

[30]G Thils, *Les laïcs dans le nouveau code de droit canonique et au IIe Concile de Vatican*, Louvain, 1983, 50

[31]A Feuillet, "Les sacrifices spirituels du sacerdoce royal des baptisés, 1 Pet 2:5", *Nouvelle Revue Théologique*, 96, 1974, 727

[32]*Old Testament Priests and the New Priest*, St Bede's Publications, Petersham, 1986

[33]Ibid., 270

[34]Ibid., 270

[35]Ibid., 271

[36]Many other authors have likewise opposed Elliot's stand. Cf. E Selwyn, *The First Epistle of St Peter*, Macmillan, New York, 1958, 296; J N D Kelly, *The Epistles of Peter and of Jude*, Black, London, 1969, 92

[37]*Old Testament Priests and the New Priest*, St Bede's Publications, Petersham, 1986, 272

[38]"Chaque fidèle 'célèbre' le sacrifice de la messe." C Vagaggini, "La dimension sacrificielle de la communion eucharistique. Reflections théologiques et liturgiques", *Communautés et liturgié*, 69, 1987, 216

[39]Congar will employ the word "concelebrants" to speak of the laity's role in eucharist and so distinguish it from the official priest who is seen to celebrate the eucharist: "dans la participation au sacrament que célèbre le sacerdoce hièrarchique et dont la consécration baptismale constitue les fidèles légitimes concélébrants". "Structure du sacerdoce chrétien" In *La maison dieu*, 27, 1951, 85

[40]"The Catholic Epistles", *Luther's Works*, Vol. 30, ed. J Pelikan, St Louis, 1967, 55

[41]G Philips, *L'église et son mystère au deuxième Concile du Vatican. Histoire, texte et commentaire de la constitution Lumen Gentium*, Paris, 1967, I, 1.38

[42]*Lumen Gentium*, n. 10, AAS Vol. LVII 1965, 14

[43]*Presbyterorum Ordinis*, n.2, AAS Vol. LVIII, 1966, 992

[44]J Coppens, "Le sacerdoce royal: un commentaire de 1 Pet. II: 4–10", *Au service de la parole de Dieu*, (Mélanges en l'Honneur de Mgs. Charue), Gembloux, 1969, 65

[45]O Casel, *Il Mistero del Culto Cristiano*, Roma, 1960, 73
[46]S Marsili, "La liturgia momento storico della salvezza", *Anàmnesis*, Vol. I, Roma, 1974, 128
[47]S Marsili, "Partecipazione sacramentale al sacrificio di Cristo", *Rivista Liturgica*, 24, 1937, 129–132 and 273–279
[48]Ibid., 132
[49]Ibid., 129
[50]S Marsili, "La Liturgia", *Nuovo Dizionario di Liturgia*, ed. D Sartore and A M Triacca, Brescia, 1984, 732
[51]"Perché la Liturgia si celebra in un tempio reale, con sacrifici reali, e suppone un sacerdozio reale", "La liturgia, momento storico della salvezza", *Anàmnesis*, Vol. I, Roma, 1974, 131
[52]"La liturgia, momento storico della salvezza", *Anàmnesis*, Vol. I, Roma, 1974, 136
[53]"Quare ad universum Corpus Ecclesiae pertinent illudque manifestant et afficiunt", *Sacrosanctum Concilium*, n. 26, *AAS*, Vol. LVI, 1964, 107
[54]Ibid., n.6, *AAS*, Vol. LVI, 1964, 100
[55]Marsili would note here that the language of Vatican II only speaks in terms of "di prendere parte alla Liturgia". He goes on to show, however, that this activity of the laity can be expressed more forcefully. "La liturgia, momento storico della salvezza", *Anàmnesis*, Vol. I, Roma, 1974, 127
[56]*Sacrosanctum Concilium*, n. 14, *AAS*, Vol. LVI, 1964, 104
[57]*Sacrosanctum Concilium*, n. 14, ibid., 104
[58]*Sacrosanctum Concilium*. n. 49, ibid., 114

SIX

Priestly Representation and Women's Ordination

David Coffey

In late 1976 the Roman Congregation for the Doctrine of the Faith issued a statement, called technically a "declaration", accompanied by an official commentary, on the question of women's ordination, the guarded conclusion of which, delivered early (par. 5), was that "the church, in fidelity to the example of the Lord, does not consider herself authorized to admit women to priestly ordination".[1]

In this chapter we take up the question of priestly representation, which figures prominently in these documents. Exactly whom or what does the priest represent when he celebrates the liturgy, especially the eucharist? After investigating this question, we shall turn to the question of women's ordination in the light of our reflections. However, we make no pretence to treat this subject exhaustively; indeed our approach is strictly limited and our conclusions will be tentative and provisional. But in the process we shall cover some interesting ground, including the anthropological presuppositions of the current discussion. We begin, then, with the question of priestly representation.

PRIESTLY REPRESENTATION

Both the declaration and the commentary referred to above reinforce the traditional teaching that in the liturgy the priest acts *in persona Christi*, "in the person of Christ".[2] This means that he represents Christ, head of the mystical body, the church. At the same time it is recognized in these documents that he acts *in persona Ecclesiae*, "in the person of the church", inasmuch as in his capacity of official minister he represents the church.[3] Both documents make the point that it is only insofar as he represents Christ that he represents the church, and the commentary goes on to say that the declaration indicated several texts from the Second Vatican Council which clearly express this teaching. An examination of these texts, however, fails to bear this claim out, though the declaration gives also a citation from Pius XII's encyclical *Mediator Dei* which does convey this teaching.[4] What the conciliar texts, from *Lumen Gentium* and *Presbyterorum ordinis*, do clearly say is that in the liturgy the priest acts *in persona Christi*.

The declaration and the commentary, at any rate, see no conflict between the two concepts *in persona Christi* and *in persona Ecclesiae*: they understand the latter in function of the former. The *Mediator Dei* text explains how this is so: "The minister of the altar represents the person of Christ as the Head, offering in the name of all his members." The commentary expresses a fear in relation to allowing a primary status to *in persona Ecclesiae*: it would make the priest simply a delegate of the community.[5] It is, of course, desirable that the priest be in some sense a delegate of the community, but not *simply* such. More important is that he be called by God and appointed by legitimate authority. However, a primary status for *in persona Ecclesiae* does not necessarily lead to the feared outcome, for when the priest acts *in persona Ecclesiae* he does so as the duly commissioned minister of the church, its official representative. In this perspective it is possible to see a reversal of dependence in our two concepts, to see *in persona Christi* as a function of *in persona Ecclesiae*. The head and directive principle (*hegemenikon*) of the church is Christ. In representing the church, therefore, the priest represents Christ its head. Here the representation of Christ is reached through the representation of the church. The validity of this mutual interdependence of the two concepts stems from the inseparability of head and members in the body of Christ: he who represents the head represents the members, and he who represents the members represents the head; for head and members are united in an indissoluble bond, which is the Holy Spirit.

Edward Kilmartin explains these two different orderings as follows: "The first (*in persona Ecclesiae*) begins with what is more accessible and progresses toward what is ultimately signified; the second (*in persona Christi*) analyzes the actual process in which what is ultimately signified directs the whole process of symbolization."⁶ While this is undoubtedly correct, I prefer to explain the difference in terms of "descending" and "ascending" theology, an extension of descending and ascending christology.

"Descending theology" has as its point of departure the sphere of God and as its term the world of human beings, while "ascending theology" begins from the world of human experience and rises to the sphere of God. These two complementary ways of doing theology, each with its foundation in the New Testament, have had very different histories. The descending method, awarded a commanding position by the form given to the christological doctrines of the early church councils, has held sway until modern times, when it has begun to be replaced, or at least balanced, by the ascending method. In this scheme *in persona Christi* clearly belongs to the descending approach and *in persona Ecclesiae* to the ascending. Given magisterial conservatism, this is probably sufficient explanation of the Roman practice of awarding a primacy to *in persona Christi* over *in persona Ecclesiae*.

A valuable benefit from being able to study the same subject matter in these two different perspectives is that an element which appears as only factually present in the descending approach may be seen in the ascending approach as necessary. The best example I can give comes from my own research and centers on the role of the Holy Spirit in the incarnation. In the traditional descending christology, derived ultimately from St John's gospel, there is no essential role for the Holy Spirit in the incarnation, though the Spirit is recognized to be present to Jesus, and indeed present "without measure". But in ascending christology, based on the synoptic tradition, the Holy Spirit bestowed creatively on Jesus by the Father is the very spirit of sonship for him, anointing him only-begotten Son of God.

Something analogous can be seen in a comparison of *in persona Christi* and *in persona Ecclesiae*. In descending theology *in persona Christi* is simply a given and *in persona Ecclesiae* is its easy and automatic extension. But in ascending theology, *in persona Ecclesiae* is seen as the indispensable prerequisite and foundation of *in persona Christi*, a necessary stage towards its acquisition. And this is their original and ontological order, for, as we know from the New Testament, ascending theology is the presupposition of descending theology, not *vice versa*.

The question now arises, how best to express the relationship of *in persona Ecclesiae* and *in persona Christi* in the perspective of ascending theology. It is a question also addressed by Kilmartin, who suggests, for expressing first and second signification, the use of the verbs "denote" and "connote" respectively.⁷ It is interesting that the example he gives comes from the field of sacramental signification, in which the usual terms (though he does not employ them here) are *sacramentum* (sign), *res et sacramentum* (symbolic reality) and *res* (grace). Thus he speaks of the sacraments of initiation, baptism and confirmation, as having the initial signification of "incorporation into the community", and this in turn functioning "to symbolize a spiritual reality: integration into the Body of Christ by the gift of the Spirit". He concludes that "what is *denoted* by the sensible rite also *connotes* a spiritual reality". This terminology is then transferred to the present question with the following conclusion: "the priest first represents (denotes) the Church in its sacramental activity and secondly represents (connotes) Christ the Head of the Church."

I agree with what Kilmartin is saying here, but would rather find terms other than "denote" and "connote", which normally are used not of persons or things but only of words and their meanings. Further, "connote" is somewhat weak, in that it does not necessarily convey the necessary link which exists between the signifier and the second significate in this instance (or in sacramental signification either). Hence I prefer "first" and "second" (rather than "secondary", in which also, the above-mentioned necessary connection suffers) "signification".[8] Equally, "direct" and "indirect representation" is suitable, and is the terminology I shall use from now on in this chapter.

The significance of the insight that the priest's representation of Christ is indirect rather than direct becomes apparent when the point is made that *in persona Ecclesiae* conceptually includes "by virtue of apostolic succession". If the priest acts as representative of the church, it is the "apostolic church" that he represents, which is not only the church that stands in historical and ontological continuity with that of the apostles, but the church in which the apostles, their successors the bishops, and those who assist them in their ministry bear from Christ the charge to do precisely what he, the priest, is doing now. He acts, therefore, not "in the person" but "in the name", of the apostles, *in nomine Apostolorum*, to whom he is linked through his bishop by apostolic succession. No one has ever suggested that he "represents" the apostles or any particular apostle in the way in which he represents Christ or the church, that is to say, sacramentally. The reason for this is that an apostle is never one who stands in his own right; he is to be understood purely as an emissary of Christ. In this context the word "represents" is therefore better avoided, as it only leads to confusion. If it *is* used, it is in a weaker, analogous sense, which means simply "acts by virtue of apostolic succession", that is, by a chain of legitimate commission extending back to the apostles. He is the representative of Christ and the church, but, through his bishop, he is a "successor" of the apostles. Room for the acquisition of this insight in its full character and relationships is opened up only by the realization of the indirect nature of his representation of Christ.

An objection to the thesis here being proposed is that according to the theology of St Thomas Aquinas, endorsed by both the declaration and the commentary,[9] in the eucharist, at least, the priest's representation of Christ is such that it cannot be described as indirect. Here the priest steps, as it were, into the very character of Christ, identifying himself with Christ's own words and gestures. It is almost as though at this point the mass becomes a sacred drama, with the priest playing the role of Christ.

Kilmartin rejects this objection with the following arguments.[10] First, it isolates the moment of consecration from the rest of the eucharistic prayer. Secondly, it ignores the structure of the eucharistic prayers, which are composed of a number of elements, of which the institution narrative is one certainly, but, very importantly, the epiclesis is another. Thirdly, the suggestion that the mass is a sacred drama isolates the priest as actor from the faithful as audience even when the latter participate after the manner of "live theatre".

To these observations I should like to add one of my own. An examination of the eucharistic prayers shows that even at the moment of consecration the priest does not really step into the character of Christ or play his part, even though he uses certain words and gestures of Christ. The form of this part of the mass is not drama; it is narrative, in which the priest speaks throughout of Christ in the third person, clearly as someone other than himself, even in the pronunciation of the words of consecration. He unmistakably maintains his direct representation of the church and his identity as its minister right through the sacred action. In this he is supported by the accoutrements, the vestments he wears and the liturgical environment in which the action takes place. The bench on which the bread and wine lie is an altar, not a table. The only concession he makes to theatricality (and it is a weak and relatively insignificant one) consists in the gesture of taking the bread and the cup in his hands, as Jesus did at the Last Supper. Even raising his eyes to heaven, which occurs in the first eucharistic prayer only, does not come from any of the institution accounts in the New Testament. Jungmann tells us that it is probably an ecclesiastical expression of oblation, based on other New Testament passages, such as

Matthew 14:19 and *John* 11:41 and 17:1, which witness to general prayer gestures of Jesus, in which he was imitated by early Christians.[11]

The inescapable conclusion is that St Thomas is incorrect at this point. The priest's way of acting *in persona Christi* at the moment of consecration is not different from what it is in the rest of the eucharistic prayer. Even in the mass, therefore, and *a fortiori* in the sacrament of reconciliation (which with the eucharist is sometimes singled out for special consideration) and the other sacraments, the priest's representation of Christ when he acts *in persona Christi* remains indirect. His direct representation is of the church, and it includes his commission to celebrate the liturgy by virtue of apostolic succession.

WOMEN'S ORDINATION

The bishops, as the Second Vatican Council reiterates, are the successors of the apostles.[12] As Peter and the apostles formed the apostolic college, similarly do the pope and bishops, in succession to them, form the episcopal college.[13] Bishops become members of this college through episcopal consecration and hierarchical communion with the head and members of the college.[14] And through their bishops, indeed as their helpers, priests and deacons participate in their respectively different ways in this apostolic succession.[15] This is a brief statement of Catholic faith on this matter, as expressed by the Council. We must now see what emerges for the question of the ordination of women from a theological reflection on it in the light of the three factors which have come to the fore in this study, namely apostolic succession, representation of the church and representation of Christ.

a) In the light of apostolic succession

Our statement uncritically assumes that the apostles are to be identified without further ado as the twelve disciples whose names are listed in the three synoptic gospels and the book of *Acts*. It was the evangelist Luke who first made this simple identification. However, Paul, in *1 Corinthians* 15:5–7, a very early witness, appears to distinguish them, and modern biblical scholarship discerns a still more complex picture. In giving a summary account of this, we begin with the question of the twelve.

No one will deny that Jesus gathered around himself an intimate group of disciples. Mark tells us (*Mark* 3:14–15) that their main function was "to be with him", but to this are added the words "to be sent out to preach and have authority to cast out demons". Whether their number was actually twelve or whether this figure was arrived at only after the resurrection on the basis of the symbolism of the twelve tribes of Israel is disputed, but Raymond Brown favors the first alternative on the grounds that: the gospels attribute to Jesus the choice of the twelve disciples; the felt need to fill the gap created by the defection of Judas points clearly in this direction; Paul (1 Corinthians 15:5) mentions that one of the earliest appearances of the risen Jesus was to the twelve; and finally, the idea of an eschatological community patterned on the tribal system of Israel was already current in Jesus' time, as is known from Qumran.[16] While not certain, this view emerges as the more likely one. We know from Q (cf. Matthew 19:28 and Luke 22:30), a very early stratum of tradition, that the purpose of the twelve, based on the symbolism of the tribes, was to represent a renewed, eschatological people of God.

The concept of an apostle is quite different. It is generally accepted that the twelve were not known as apostles during the ministry of Jesus. The concept arose only after, and as a result of, the resurrection. An apostle was one sent by the risen Jesus to bear witness to his resurrection. According to Paul, this involved a vision of the risen Jesus and a commission by him to preach. The apostles were originally a wider group than the twelve, and included Paul, James the brother of the Lord, and Barnabas. However, the twelve were the most obvious candidates for this role. Their intimacy with their master equipped them above all others to bear witness to the Jesus tradition and to judge post-resurrection developments by it. Drawing on tradition, Paul reports in 1 Corinthians 15:5 that they were among the first to see the risen Jesus. One can easily understand Luke's efforts to restrict the title to them.

With the exception of Peter, however, it is not clear that any members of the twelve functioned outside Jerusalem. The model of the later traveling apostle was Paul, and his example determined the further development of the concept. Already in the New Testament it is probable that it expanded to include those associated with the ministry of the original apostles, even though they had not themselves received a direct vision or commission from the risen Jesus. That, certainly, is the concept which obtains in the Didache (ch.11), dated about mid-second century.

From this we can conclude that of the three logical stages here considered, the second, that is, that in which the apostle is understood as one commissioned by Jesus to preach the resurrection, is the determinative one. This had no connection with the twelve as such. Development took place in two directions: first backwards, that is, in a logical if not temporal order, to include the twelve as the apostles *par excellence*, and then forwards, in an order clearly both logical and temporal, to embrace those associated with the mission of the original holders of the office.

In the light of this conclusion we need to clarify what exactly is meant by "apostolic succession". To whom do new office-bearers succeed, the twelve or the apostles, and if the latter, to which group in the different stages of the development of the concept? It is clear that it was not possible to succeed to the twelve as such. They were, and remain, unique. They exercise a foundational and eschatological role that is unrepeatable. The replacement of Judas by Matthias (*Acts* 1:15–26) constitutes no objection to this. Judas did not just die; he defected from the faith. He did not even begin to exercise his foundational role, nor did he receive an appearance of the risen Jesus. The exercise of replacement was not repeated when James of Zebedee was martyred in the Herodian persecution (*Acts* 12:2), nor when any other members of the twelve died.

Brown states that "the bishops became the successors of the apostles by taking over the pastoral care of the churches the traveling apostles had established—this is the most verifiable understanding of 'apostolic succession'."[17] However, he also directs attention to an essay of Lucien Cerfaux according to which "for theological purposes of church constitution and order we should concentrate on the collegiate concept of the Twelve as a body."[18] The thesis of the essay is that "the Twelve were, and remain, the basic element and support of the more extended 'apostolic' college. They confer their dignity on it. The enlarged college did not essentially change the physiognomy of the restricted college of the Twelve, and it participates in its privileges."[19]

These contrasting statements of Brown and Cerfaux are reconciled only by recognizing a tendency towards reabsorption, not only of the apostles into the twelve as already noted, but of the traveling (or "itinerant") apostles into the original apostles and thence into the twelve. Corresponding to the *historical* movement of devolution from the twelve through the apostles to the traveling apostles was an opposite *theological* movement of assimilation of the traveling apostles through the apostles back to the twelve.

However, Cerfaux speaks too sweepingly when he says that the apostolic college did not change the physiognomy of the college of the twelve and that it participates in its privileges. It could not participate in anything that was unique to the twelve as such. Perhaps we can say that, apart from the prestige of the twelve, it participates in only one of their prerogatives, namely their collegiate character, and so, as continued by the bishops, that is, as the episcopal college (with the pope at its head), it becomes the organ of unity in the church (the Holy Spirit being the principle of this unity).

In nothing that has been said here about apostolic succession does a reason emerge for the exclusion of women from it. Perhaps an argument could be constructed if the apostolic and episcopal colleges inherited the foundational and eschatological function of the twelve. Then perhaps it could be said that the representative role of these colleges required their members to be male so as to correspond to the patriarchs of Israel. But then it would probably also have to be insisted that the membership of each college be restricted to twelve! In any case, as we have seen, the foundational and eschatological function is proper to the twelve and cannot be passed on to later groups. As we also saw, those who act in the apostolic succession do not represent the apostles; they merely act in their name. In some feminist writing the contention has been popularized that one of the traveling apostles mentioned in the New Testament was in fact a woman. The reference is to Romans 16:7, which, translated "neutrally", reads: "Greet Andronicus and Junia, my kinsfolk and fellow prisoners; they are persons of note among the apostles, and they were in Christ before me." It appears to be established that the second name mentioned here is "Junia", which is feminine, and not "Junias", which would be masculine.[20] However, the sentence itself is ambiguous and does not admit of a convincing resolution. It could mean either that Andronicus and Junia were apostles of note, or that they were non-apostles regarded by the apostles as persons of note.

b) In the light of representation of the church

We now move on to reflect on our statement of faith in the light of the second factor, the priest's representation of the church.

First it needs to be clarified whether the expression in persona Ecclesiae primarily denotes the whole church, head and members, or just the visible or earthly church. Scripture and tradition approve the drawing of this distinction. The whole church is the mystical body of Christ; its personal symbol is Jesus Christ himself; and in this conception the church is grasped over against God, that is, the Father. The earthly church, on the other hand, is the community of the redeemed, the bride of Christ; its personal symbol is Mary; and it is grasped over against Christ, its redeemer.[21] I wish to argue now that the word "Ecclesiae" in the expression *in persona Ecclesiae* primarily refers to the earthly church.

The argument is based on the concept just considered, namely, apostolic succession. The very first reason the priest has for assuming the presidential role in the liturgy is that he is commissioned for this by virtue of apostolic succession. He is invested with the legitimate credentials and authority to be there and to act thus, and his legitimation comes from his bishop and ultimately from the apostles. Why not ultimately from Christ? Because the church as such exists only after, and as a result of, the resurrection, by which Christ is removed from earth to heaven. He remains with the church of course, but in the Spirit, not the flesh. It is for the *apostles* to bind and loose on earth, and it is their decisions that are ratified in heaven. And further, these decisions become, by reception, decisions of the whole church on earth.

The church in whose name, therefore, the priest acts when he celebrates the liturgy is the apostolic church, the church whose nucleus is the episcopal college and which by apostolic succession is one with the church whose nucleus was the apostolic college. This church says to him not only, "Act in our name," but "Represent us to your community". It can also say, "Act in the name of Christ", for its authority comes from Christ. But it cannot say, "Represent Christ to your community", because it is the servant of Christ, not his master. Authority can be passed on from person to person, but the power to represent has to be granted directly by the person or community to be represented. However, the priest does represent Christ to the community, and for the reason stated earlier: because of the indissoluble bond which exists between the head and the members of the church, namely, the Holy Spirit, he who represents the members represents Christ the head. Finally, it is thus, that is, as representative of the members and representative of the head, that he represents the whole church, head and members.

I therefore postulate the following logical (not temporal) order in the priest's representation. First he acts *in persona Ecclesiae* where "Ecclesiae" means the earthly church; then he acts *in persona Christi*, where "Christi" designates Christ the head of the church; and finally he acts in a way that can be named either *in persona Ecclesiae* or *in persona Christi*, where "Ecclesiae" and "Christi" each has the same material designation, namely, the whole church or the whole Christ, head and members. Because these designations, the earthly church, Christ and the whole church, are inseparably connected, there is no inconsistency when the liturgy has the priest pass from one representation to another, as happens in the eucharistic prayers. What moves is just the emphasis, from one of these intrinsically linked designations to another. However, the priest's primary and direct representation is of the earthly church, and it is only insofar as he represents it that he is able to represent Christ and the whole church.

Nothing said above leads to the conclusion that the earthly church cannot be represented by a woman. As a community comprising both men and women the church could be represented by either a man or a woman. But in fact the personal symbol of the earthly church is a woman, Mary. As the one *intuitu meritorum Filii sui sublimiore modo redempta*, the one "redeemed in a more exalted fashion by reason of the merits of her Son", as the Second Vatican Council calls her,[22] Mary is the obvious personal symbol of the earthly church, the community of those redeemed by Christ. Further, her femaleness allows her in her person to express in bridal symbolism, as does the New Testament, the covenant relationship which exists between the church and Christ. However, a woman representing the church would not reflect Mary, for she would also have to represent Christ, and the same person, being of one sex only, could not simultaneously represent both the bride and the bridegroom. Therefore the femaleness of the woman representative would only symbolize the essential feminine character (about which more will be said later), not the bridal character, of the church. Because of his sex, a man would be less capable, but not incapable, of expressing in his person the feminine character of the church. This is so because of the fluidity of masculine and feminine characteristics, as we shall see later also. Though he can still represent the church, therefore, a man does so in a weaker way than could a woman. We conclude that there is nothing forbidding the representation of the earthly church by a woman; on the contrary, in the context of Christian symbolism a woman can do it better than a man.

An important corollary to be drawn from these reflections is that, as the priest acts both *in persona Ecclesiae* and *in persona Christi*, the symbolism that applies here cannot be that of bride and bridegroom united in covenant. And if this symbolism is ruled out on the side of the church, it is ruled out also on the side of Christ. We are left, then, with just one functioning set of symbols, namely, the members and the head of the mystical body.

c) In the light of representation of Christ

We are thus brought to the last aspect under which we wish to reflect on our statement of faith, the priest's representation of

But the church doesn't rule its indirect.

So say you?

Christ. It will be useful to reiterate at the outset a conclusion arrived at earlier, that is, that the priest's representation of Christ is via his representation of the church and is therefore indirect. In the process of reaching this conclusion the Thomistic theology of a direct representation of Christ in the case of the eucharist was ruled out.

An argument can be constructed immediately from premises already available. The major is established: he who represents the members of the mystical body can represent Christ its head. And we have seen that a woman can represent the members, inasmuch as she can represent the earthly church. Therefore a woman can represent Christ the head. The principle, therefore, should be reworded: he *or she* who represents the members can represent the head. Some would reject this argument on the grounds that it contradicts the Pauline ruling that only a man can exercise headship (cf. *1 Corinthians* 11:3; *Ephesians* 5:23). But Pope John Paul II himself, commenting on the *Ephesians* text, has justly called this idea a "concept rooted in the mentality of the times", and interpreted the text in the light of the introductory verse (*Ephesians* 5:21) which calls on all Christians without differentiation "to be subject to each other out of reverence for Christ".[23] There seems, then, to be no valid objection against a woman exercising headship as such in the church, this headship being understood, of course, as a participation in, and representation of, that of Christ.

This argument is supported by a consideration of the concepts "image of God" and "image of Christ". The text of *Genesis* 1:26-7, "Then God said, 'Let us make man in our image, after our likeness;... So God created man in his own image; in the image of God he created him; male and female he created them'," has had a theological impact well beyond its literal sense. Most likely, the "image of God" was meant to indicate only the vicarious divine authority which humankind would wield over the rest of creation, and the mention of male and female was to manifest God's intention that they should perpetuate themselves by propagation.[24]

However, when the New Testament speaks of Christ as the perfect image of God (*Philippians* 2:6; *Colossians* 1:15; *Hebrews* 1:3), far more than this is meant. Likewise, when Christians are said to be in turn "the image of Christ" (*Romans* 8:29; *1 Corinthians* 15:49; *Colossians* 3:10; *1 John* 3:2), it is their supreme dignity in regard to Christ and to God that is being affirmed. It is important to note that these texts make no differentiation between men and women. They are equally the image of Christ. And in that case both men and women can represent Christ. We cannot say that they could *equally* represent him, as some other factor may intervene to invalidate such a statement.

It remains now to consider what Gerald Gleeson has characterized as "what seems to be the strongest argument offered thus far for the exclusion of women from the ordained ministry",[25] namely, the argument from nuptial imagery. This argument, of course, we have already excluded in principle, but it is important even so to examine it in its actual formulation and presuppositions. It is invoked by both the declaration and the commentary.[26] The argument concedes that a woman can represent Christ, but it denies that she can represent him precisely in the role of bridegroom, that is, of the church. And this role, it is claimed, is exercised by the priest in the celebration of the liturgy.

It is not possible to proceed with a discussion of this argument at any depth without first considering, and taking a stand on, the current debate about Christian anthropology, and so it is to this subject that we now turn. An important preliminary is to point out that the terms "male" and "female" denote the biological distinction of the sexes, while "masculine" and "feminine" have to do with the psychological and spiritual characteristics traditionally associated respectively with males, for example, rationality, assertiveness and independence, and with females, for example, bodiliness, sensitivity, relationality and nurturing qualities.[27]

Anne Carr sums up the contemporary discussion by presenting three current models of Christian anthropology.[28] The first, called "dual anthropology", makes a comprehensive distinction between the sexes along physical, psychological and spiritual lines, and sees this all-encompassing distinction as given by God with nature and therefore as unchangeable. The second, "single anthropology", recognizes as unchangeable only the biological differences, regarding the others as requiring to be overcome, and so places the emphasis on culture rather than nature. The third, called "transformative anthropology", "transforms the old gender stereotypes at the same time that it aims to transform the social and cultural structures that are their inseparable context in human life".[29] To the obvious question, as to how the third model differs from the second, the answer is given that, whereas models one and two are actual historical models reflecting the shortcomings of their respective geneses, model three represents a liberating challenge for the future.[30] However, while this may be so, it does not appear to add anything to the second by way of content. I propose, therefore, that we can accept that in fact the current discussion offers us a choice of two models, the dual and the single anthropology.

It is undeniable, however, that each of these anthropologies is seriously flawed. One can only sympathize with the effort to find a third, more acceptable way. I shall not rehearse here the detailed criticisms of them which Carr assembles; rather, I shall simply offer a brief general critique out of which a suggestion of my own will emerge.

The basic problem with each of them is that for the case of humanity they make too sharp a distinction between nature and culture. The first places too strong an emphasis on nature, the second too strong an emphasis on culture. But if one accepts the general anthropology of Karl Rahner, which Carr does, one is ineluctably led to a blurring of this distinction, or at least to the inclusion of culture within nature. If in the infrapersonal world nature is taken as fixed and determined, it is clear that the term can only be used of human beings in an analogous sense; for thanks to culture, nature for them is something essentially plastic. In other words, if human nature is grasped as self-transcendence towards God actualized in experience in the world, culture, as that which forms and in turn is formed by this experience, becomes a dimension of this "nature" itself. It is not something added on to it, or even a medium external to it through which it attains some kind of subsequent expression. This means that even though nature, as created, is finite and in a sense fixed, it is at the same time self-transcendent and open to endless change. It is the *finitum capax infiniti*, the finite capable of the infinite. This tension within the human being is rooted in its composite character, that is, in the fact that it is made up of matter and spirit.

This leads us to distinguish three kinds of human characteristics. The first lies firmly on the side of matter, and has to do with the fixed physical being of humans. Here sexual differentiation plays a crucial part and results in, not two natures, but two complementary forms of the same nature, as in the animal kingdom where physical complementarity is ordered towards reproduction and nurturing. The third lies just as firmly on the side of spirit and is therefore psychological and spiritual and "neutral", possessable equally by males and females. The second category is situated somewhere in between. It is psychological and spiritual but rooted in the physical. Analogous to instincts in animals, it is nevertheless fully human. Therefore at this level also there is complementarity, and it issues in separate masculine and feminine characteristics, examples of which we listed earlier. But this is not to say it is set in concrete, for being spiritual it is open to acquisition by all. Being human is therefore a challenge, to develop and direct that with which nature has endowed us and to acquire what it has not, so that a balance is achieved both in ourselves and in society.

It would be hard to "prove" a philosophical anthropology, but it is possible at least to indicate points in its favor. Against both the dual and the single anthropology the charge of dualism can, in respectively different ways, be leveled, but I do not think it can be brought against what I am proposing here. At least my suggested anthropology takes "embodiedness" seriously. But at the same time it does not permit a rigid and comprehensive distinction between the sexes which can, and in the past did, allow and promote the subordination of women to men. Also, my anthropology recognizes the validity of masculine and feminine characteristics and encourages men to be masculine and women to be feminine without condoning either chauvinism among men or manipulative dependence among women. At the same time too it holds out the challenge of achieving full humanity to both men and women, but in, to use one of Rahner's favorite words, an "asymptotic" way. That is to say, given the complementarity of the sexes, the tension of endowment and challenge in each person allows the goal of full humanity to be achieved by each only in part. This seems a more modest and practical objective than that held out by the single anthropology. My anthropology could well be called "transformative", but not in the sense of Carr's third model, since asymptoticality is of its essence.

Students of this subject will be well aware that this anthropology is supported by the psychology of Jung, and that Jung himself has been strongly criticized by some feminists on the grounds that the complementarity he affirms only allows and encourages the continued subordination of women to men. In Elizabeth Johnson's words, they see it as "a patriarchal invention based on a profoundly dualistic anthropology which stereotypes women and constricts them to predetermined, politically powerless roles".[31]

However, if this anthropology can be used as a weapon by men against women in the battle of the sexes, that is not to say that it has to be used in this way. It may well be true in itself. One is reminded of Roger Garaudy's observation on Marx's atheism, namely, that it is "methodological" rather than "metaphysical". Garaudy wrote: "His atheism is not metaphysical but methodological, one that dismisses the 'God of the gaps' and the 'God of alibis'. Today, many Christians are integrating this radical critique into their faith as one of its most important elements, because they are aware that 'methodological atheism' may be the best defence of God's honor".[32] The rejection of Jungian complementarity by some feminists appears likewise to be methodological rather than metaphysical. While understandable as a short-term tactic, it is hardly defensible in the long-term interests of truth.

For the sake of greater clarity, I would now like to formulate the anthropological question in terms of two concepts of which Gleeson also takes account, that is to say, "donative" and "receptive".[33] These terms, which are not to be confused with "active" and "passive", can serve as general descriptions of masculine and feminine characteristics respectively, and like them are open to appropriation by either sex. As was said earlier, these characteristics are rooted in the physical differentiation of the sexes. Hence I fully endorse Gleeson's statement that "in view of the structure of the sexual act, and the fact that it is the woman who 'receives' and carries the child a couple conceive, the *symbolic* description of the two spouses as donative and receptive seems undeniable."[34] The problem with the dual anthropology was that it generalized and extended this donativity and receptivity respectively into almost every department of life, while the problem with the single anthropology is that it attempts to restrict them to the physical sphere alone.

In my suggested anthropology they are endorsed at the physical level and also at the level of differentiated masculine and feminine characteristics, but at the same time it is recognized that at this and at the higher level of undifferentiated characteristics men can and should be receptive as well as donative and women can and should be donative as well as receptive.

Thus we can resume our final task, a consideration of the argument from nuptial imagery. Does the priest in the celebration of the liturgy, particularly the eucharist, represent Christ precisely as bridegroom of the church? If this question is answered in the affirmative, that would be the end of the road for the prospect of women's ordination, for we would be dealing with a male quality, not just a masculine quality that could be appropriated by women. It is different for a man representing the church in its feminine quality: this can be done precisely because the quality in this case is feminine rather than female. To those who object that a purely symbolic reality such as this should not be allowed to stand in the way of women's ordination, Gleeson's words should be brought home: "A longstanding prejudice would subordinate the symbolical to the ontological. However, in the realm of the sacramental, ontology and essence are constituted by symbolic meaning. Symbolism is no added decoration."[35]

Even in secular life, then, symbols are much more important than is usually allowed.[36] But in the field of religion symbols are even more important. As Gleeson, again, observes, "It is precisely through the contingency and superfluity of symbols and rituals that religions evoke the transcendent, the gratuity of Divine presence and absence".[37]

It is not clear, however, that in the liturgy the priest does represent Christ as the bridegroom of the church. John Donahue asserts, "In the New Testament the image (of bridegroom and bride) is used only of Christ and the Church and never extended into the area of ministry".[38] The statement of the Anglican–Roman Catholic Dialogue in the United States on Christian anthropology is more nuanced. While, like Donahue, it rejects the idea that any allusion to the nuptial mystery in relation to the eucharist is explicit in the New Testament, it admits that there are such allusions in the celebration of the eucharist in the church.[39]

Is it, then, a matter of implicit allusions in the New Testament becoming explicit in the liturgy? Jeremias characterizes the meals which Jesus shared with publicans and sinners as "eschatological", as "anticipatory celebrations of the feast in the end-time".[40] And Schillebeeckx alerts us, "Although it is a separate tradition, we must not see the Last Supper as wholly detached from the many instances during Jesus' earthly life when he made the offer of salvation through the shared meal of fellowship".[41] It is considerations such as these, reworked and synthesized in the light of the resurrection, that underlie the exclamation, "Happy are those who are invited to the marriage supper of the Lamb" (*Revelation* 19:9), where this meal, at which Jesus himself is the paterfamilias, is the eschatological fulfillment of heaven, and nuptial imagery, depicting the covenant relationship between himself and the church, is introduced for the first time. The link with the eucharist, though implicit, is undeniable. And it is this text, in combination with *John* 1:29, which is alluded to in the priest's invitation to the faithful to receive holy communion at mass: "This is the Lamb of God who takes away the sins of the world. Happy are those who are called to his supper." It could perhaps be argued that something implicit in Scripture has here become explicit in tradition.

This suggestion cannot be dismissed out of hand, particularly as, as Rahner remarks, "we really have no clear answer . . . to the problem of how to distinguish in principle between a 'divine' tradition and a generally and long-enduring 'human' tradition".[42] However, there are persuasive considerations on the other side, which we now present.

It should first be pointed out that the example just given only dates from the time of the post-Vatican II reform, and that its text only has the status of an option. The General Instruction of the Roman Missal only requires that the priest invite the faithful "to participate in the meal ... using words from the gospel".[43] But there are weightier considerations also.

We have already established that in the liturgy the priest represents Christ as head of the mystical body. Apart from the fact that this is solidly attested by the magisterium, it is the necessary link between the priest's representation of the church and his representation of Christ, as we have also shown. I now wish to make the point that insofar as he represents the one person, Christ, under one particular symbol, it is not possible for the priest simultaneously to represent him under another symbol. It is not possible, therefore, for him simultaneously to represent Christ as head of the mystical body and as bridegroom of the church. Admittedly, *allusion* is made to this second symbol in the liturgy, but the *representation* remains consistent, namely, of Christ as head. I would here use the word "allusion" in the same sense as I have used "connotation" in counter-distinction to Kilmartin. Admittedly, this allusion is more telling when made by a man, but it could also be made by a woman. The United States dialogue document already referred to seems to reflect a similar view when it says of some Episcopalians, "It does not seem to them that it (this allusion) should apply to the celebrant of the eucharist, at least in such a way as to necessitate the restriction of holy orders to men".[44]

The church's actual practice tends to confirm the view that allusion rather than representation is the operative concept here. The church is consistent in carrying through the representation of Christ's headship from the liturgy into its daily life, and so has resisted pleas to separate the power of jurisdiction from that of orders in order to give women a greater voice in its affairs. And in this it is supported by sound theology, which is loath to interpret jurisdiction juridically, preferring to grasp it in sacramental terms, in which it really cannot be separated from orders. But no comparable consistency is detectable in the matter of signifying Christ as bridegroom. Priests belonging to Eastern rites of the Catholic church are permitted to be married; and, although it is sometimes asserted that bishops are "married" to their local churches, no problem is felt in transferring a bishop from one diocese to another if this is thought to be in the interests of the wider church. It is clear, then, that the church itself does not put signification of Christ as bridegroom on the same level as representation of Christ as head.

It is, of course, a fact that in his dynamic relationship to the church Christ is donative and the church receptive. We already allowed that a woman can represent the church in its feminine quality of receptivity better than a man. It can be objected here that, as we refer to the reception of spiritual realities, of which men too stand in need, we stereotype women when we associate this kind of receptivity in a special way with them. But here again, as with Jungian complementarity, it would seem to be a matter of tactics rather than truth. Once we recognize that receptivity is the clear distinguishing mark of women only at the physical level and that human characteristics at the psychological and spiritual levels are appropriable by each sex (though the feminine ones flow more readily out of women's natural endowment), it seems quite acceptable, for symbolic purposes, to characterize receptivity in a general way as feminine. That is why we maintained earlier that a woman can represent the church better than a man. It is what the church has traditionally done through its Marian doctrine, without, I claim, committing itself to a dual anthropology. By the same token, it is appropriate to characterize donativity in a general way as masculine. While the priest does not represent the maleness of Christ, he does represent the masculinity, in that in his role of minister he represents him in his donativity. Therefore, a man represents Christ better than a woman.

Thus, the priest represents Christ because he first represents the church; and a woman can represent the church better than a man; but a man can represent Christ better than a woman. In regard to their total representative ability, there appears to be little to choose between a man and a woman. Either can represent Christ and the church; neither does so perfectly. The reason is that, of the two beings to be represented, one is essentially masculine in character, the other essentially feminine. A single person, because of the fluidity of masculine and feminine characteristics, can represent both; but because this person necessarily belongs to one sex rather than the other, he or she cannot represent both perfectly.

CONCLUSION

It has always been recognized that in celebrating the liturgy the priest represents both the church and Christ. He acts both *in persona Ecclesiae* and *in persona Christi*. It is possible to read off the former as a function of the latter, and indeed this is what traditionally has been done. Without denying the validity of this, we have shown in this chapter that a more fundamental approach requires us to reverse this order. In approaching the matter in this new way, we are enabled to incorporate apostolic succession in our scheme, and understand how the priest acts also *in nomine Apostolorum.*

Turning our attention to women's ordination, we then asked how this question is affected by our findings concerning apostolic succession, representation of the church and representation of Christ. We found no bar to women's ordination presented by the first two of these considerations. The third was more difficult. Though overall it did not appear to offer any serious objection either, it raised the question of a possible divine tradition to the contrary. This would have to be investigated further; but it needs to be remembered that the bare existence and antiquity of a tradition are not enough to constitute an argument. Whether it is eventually judged divine or human will depend on the uncovering and full revelation of its underlying grounds. I hope we have contributed here to the beginning of this task.

[1]Sacred Congregation for the Doctrine of the Faith, "Declaration on the Question of the Admission of Women to the Ministerial Priesthood", 15 October, 1976, *Origins,* Vol. 6, no. 33, 3 Feb., 1977, 517–24. "A Commentary on the Declaration" appeared simultaneously, and was published in the same number of *Origins,* 524–31
[2]Cf. Declaration, par. 26, and Commentary, pars. 39–44. The expression was first used by St Paul, in *II Corinthians* 2:10
[3]Cf. Declaration, par. 32, and Commentary, par. 44
[4]Declaration, note 21
[5]Cf. Commentary, par. 44
[6]E Kilmartin, "Bishop and Presbyter as Representatives of the Church and Christ", *Women priests: a Catholic Commentary on the Vatican Declaration,* (eds. L Swidler and A Swidler), Paulist Press, New York, 1977, 296. Brackets added.
[7]Cf. Kilmartin, ibid., 296–8
[8]For the same reason I think "denote" could be used in both instances, though of course in that case no distinction would be made or relationship expressed.
[9]Cf. Declaration, par. 26, and Commentary, par. 41
[10]Cf. Kilmartin, n. 6 above, 299–300
[11]Cf. Jungmann, *The Mass of the Roman Rite,* Vol. 2, Benziger Brothers, New York, 1955, 198
[12]Cf. *Lumen Gentium,* art. 18
[13]Cf. ibid., art. 22
[14]Cf. ibid
[15]Cf. ibid., art. 20
[16]Cf. Raymond Brown, "The Twelve and the Apostolate", *The New Jerome Biblical Commentary,* eds. R Brown, J Fitzmyer and R Murphy, Prentice Hall, Englewood Cliffs, NJ, 1990, 1377–81
[17]Ibid., 1381
[18]Ibid
[19]"... les Douze furent et restent l'élément de base et le support du collège 'apostolique' plus étendu. Ils lui confèrent leur dignité. Le collège élargi n'a donc pas changé essentiellement la physionomie du collège restreint des Douze et il participe à ses privilèges." L. Cerfaux, "L'unité du Corps apostolique dans le Nouveau Testament", *Recueil Lucien Cerfaux,* vol. 2, Éditions J Duculot S A, Gembloux, 1954, 229

20Cf. Bernadette Brooten, "Junia... Outstanding among the Apostles" (*Romans* 16:7), *Woman Priests*, n. 6 above 141-4

21By the expression "the earthly church" we do not mean to exclude the saints in heaven or the suffering in purgatory; we intend simply the church *over against* Christ, i.e., the church in union with Christ, but as not including him.

22*Lumen Gentium*, art. 53

23Pope John Paul II, "Deeper Understanding of the Church and Marriage", *L'Osservatore Romano*, 24-30 August, 1982, 3, par. 5; cf. also "Reverence for Christ the Basis for Relationship between Spouses", *L'Osservatore Romano*, 16-23 August, 1982, 1, 16

24Cf. Richard Clifford, "Genesis", *The New Jerome Biblical Commentary*, eds. R Brown, J Fitzmyer and R Murphy, Prentice Hall, Englewood Cliffs, NJ, 1990, 11

25Gerald Gleeson, "The Ordination of Women and the Symbolism of Priesthood, Part I", *The Australasian Catholic Record*, 67, 1990, 473

26Cf. Declaration, pars. 29 and 30, and Commentary, par. 45

27Cf. Elizabeth Johnson, "Mary and the Face of God", *Theological Studies*, 50, 1989, 517

28Cf. Anne Carr, *Transforming Grace*, Harper and Row, San Francisco, 1988, 117-33

29Carr, ibid., 127

30Cf. Carr, ibid., 127-8

31Johnson, "Mary and the Female Face of God", 517

32Roger Garaudy, *The Alternative Future*, Pelican Books, Harmondsworth, 1976, 88

33Cf. Gleeson, "The Ordination of Women and the Symbolism of Priesthood", n. 25 above, 480

34Gleeson, ibid

35Gleeson, ibid., 477. At the author's request I have made corrections to this quotation.

36For example, the republican movement in Australia is often dismissed as unimportant on the grounds that for Australia the British crown is *only* symbolic. It is overlooked that this symbol continues powerfully to impede the formation of an authentic sense of Australian identity.

37Gleeson, ibid., Part II, *The Australasian Catholic Record*, 68, 1991, 83

38John Donahue, "A Tale of Two Documents", *Women Priests*, n. 6 above, 29. Brackets added.

39Cf. Anglican-Roman Catholic Dialogue in the United States, "Images of God: Reflections on Christian Anthropology", *Origins*, Vol. 13, no. 30, 5 Jan., 1984, par. 66

40Cf. Joachim Jeremias, *The Proclamation of Jesus* (New Testament Theology, Vol. 1), SCM Press, London, 1971, 116

41E Schillebeeckx, *Jesus—An Experiment in Christology*, Collins, London, 1979, 307

42Karl Rahner, "Women and the Priesthood", *Theological Investigations*, vol. 20, Darton, Longman and Todd, London, 1981, 46

43*The Roman Missal*, E J Dwyer, Sydney, 1974, p. xxxiii

44Anglican-Roman Catholic Dialogue, "Images of God", see n. 39 above, par. 66

SEVEN

The Priest as a Moral Guide

Neil Brown

Franz Jägerstätter, an Austrian farmer, was executed at the command of a military court on August 9, 1943, for his refusal to serve in the German Army. He had become a conscientious objector to the war because of his conviction that the Nazi regime was evil, its war unjust, and that to support either was contrary to his Catholic faith. He was counselled against this stand by the then resident priest in his village of St Radegund, other priests he consulted, and also by the local bishop at Linz: they argued that his duty to his wife and family should come first; that as a private citizen he was not responsible for the acts and policies of the government; that he lacked the 'competence', the 'information' and the 'right' to challenge governmental authority, and that he should therefore follow its orders as a loyal citizen. After the war his bishop is reported to have said of him:

> All respect is due the innocently erroneous conscience; it will have its reward from God. For the instruction of *men*, the better models are to be found in the example set by the heroes who conducted themselves "consistently" in the light of a clear and correct conscience.[1]

To the calmer gaze of a later time the mixture of compromise, fear, institutional blindness, paternalism and, at the same time, genuine pastoral concern to save the man's life and spare his family, is all too evident in this account. What was then unhesitatingly considered to be 'erroneous' has now tended

101

to move into the category of objectively right and what was regarded as 'clear and correct conscience' has slipped into the more tenuous range of the subjectively erroneous.

This movement over time from one judgment to another should alert us to the changes, sometimes very subtle, but still significant, that may occur in moral consciousness within a given tradition in response to new circumstances or as a result of new insights. Vocabulary may give the appearance of stability, and usually does, but under the surface, within the moral concepts, criteria may be changing, strong impulses may be coming from the core of the tradition that will lead to a shift in priorities, or new historical challenges may be demanding a different response. Often it is a case of all such factors combining to form new moral judgments, better suited to the altered situation. This has certainly occurred over the past few decades with regard to the Christian attitude to war. Pacificism is now viewed as a legitimate, and even at times a very desirable, prophetic option. The destructive potential of modern weaponry has stringently curtailed the legitimating conditions for a 'just' war. Individual responsibility is given a much more prominent place. And certain forms of behavior, such as chemical warfare, mass bombing, and indiscriminate attacks on civilians, are absolutely forbidden. The moral climate of the Catholic tradition on this issue thus appears now very different from what it was formerly.[2]

I

Traditionally, the relationship of Catholics to those in authority in the church has been defined in terms of "submission" to its teaching and "obedience" to one's superiors. Both these terms therefore must be critically examined before a better understanding can be achieved of both how the church should function internally as a moral community formed in the spirit of the gospel and how a Christian ethic can be fostered that is authentically responsive to the rapidly changing conditions of the modern world. One cannot escape the impression that the traditional portrayal, with its hierarchical relationships and fixed moral categories, is more suited to earlier times than to our own. A model that depicts the authority, whether pope, bishop, priest or religious superior, as having all the answers and the rest of the church as being required only to submit and to obey, is becoming increasingly difficult to sustain, if not from authority's side, then certainly in the view of many lay people. The best of the traditional teaching, however, did preserve a personal space for the subject confronted by the precepts and declarations of numerous superiors both ecclesiastical and civil. This space has been highlighted in more recent times as respect for the rights of individual conscience. How one considers the role of conscience in the church will determine the precise way the priest should function as a moral guide in the parish community. The first step then is to look at the traditional position more closely, before attempting a redescription of the way the role might be exercised.

The decision of the Congregation for the Clergy in *The Washington Case* (April 26, 1971) states that those exercising diocesan faculties are assumed to intend to communicate the teaching of the magisterium to those in their charge "according to the traditional norms of the church". The *Constitution on the Church* summed up these norms: infallible definitions of the magisterium are to "be adhered to with the submission of faith; to the ordinary magisterium is owed 'a religious assent of soul'".[3] The Council goes on to explain:

This religious submission of will and mind must be shown in a special way to the authentic teaching authority of the Roman Pontiff, even when he is not speaking *ex cathedra*. That is, it must be shown in such a way that his supreme magisterium is acknowledged with reverence, the judgments made by him are sincerely adhered to, according to his manifest mind and will. His mind and will in the matter may be known chiefly either from the character of the documents, from his frequent repetition of the same doctrine, or from his manner of speaking (25).

These norms define the precise relationship of the church community to the magisterium's role of preserving the authentic faith of the gospel. From a wider point of view, however, the primary vehicle of faith is not the magisterium, but the church as a whole: "The body of the faithful as a whole, anointed as they are by the Holy One (cf.*I John 2:20,27*), cannot err in matters of belief"(12). This is attributed to a "supernatural sense of the faith" which is characterized by a universal consensus, in the church "in matters of faith and morals". This faith, the *Constitution on Divine Revelation* states, is "committed to the church", and the magisterium's role is to interpret and defend it: it "is not above the word of God, but serves it, teaching only what has been handed on, listening to it devoutly, guarding it scrupulously, and explaining it faithfully by divine commission and with the help of the Holy Spirit" (10). What is proposed, therefore, is not a voluntarist or nominalist account of arbitrary will demanding blind obedience but a common faithfulness to the revelation entrusted to the witness of the church as a whole.

The scope of the church's infallibility traditionally includes "faith and morals" in as far as they express "the deposit of divine revelation". It is a charism exercised by the magisterium, ensuring that its definitive defense of the church's faith is free from error independently of the "consent of the church", but it too, far from being isolated from the church as a whole, is governed by the common grasp by the whole church of the revelation entrusted to it: the Council states that the magisterium should "strive painstakingly and by appropriate means to inquire properly into that revelation and to give apt expression to its contents".[4] The authority of the magisterium is taken to include all that is contained in revelation and all that is necessary for its explanation and defense, including the duty "to declare and confirm by her authority those principles of the moral order which have their origin in human nature itself".[5] Infallibility then enshrines the unfailing witness of the whole church to the full reality of its faith insofar as this is articulated in the course of history and in dialogue with different cultures. If there were then infallible pronouncements with respect to "morals", they would require the "submission of faith" due to such statements as essential elements of the authentic understanding of the faith at a given time in its development. Even so, as irreformably true, such statements would not mean the end of development, but, as integral parts of the historical understanding and articulation of faith, they would become the basis for further insight by the whole church into the revelation entrusted to it. In fact, however, the prevailing opinion of theologians is that, although traditionally extending to "morals", the church's infallibility has never been exercised in a specifically moral matter. Peter Chirico, for example, maintains:

> I do not think that any of the church's specific moral teaching of the past or present with regard to concrete moral actions has been infallibly proclaimed. I would go further; I do not believe that such specific morality can ever be infallibly proclaimed.[6]

Some have proposed that the church's teaching on contraception should be classed as irrevocable teaching,[7] but it is far from clear that such teaching even though it could be classed as "constant", has ever been proposed *definitively* as revealed faith or as necessarily connected with it.[8] Canon 749 also states that, "no doctrine is understood to be infallibly defined unless this is manifestly demonstrated". The general theological consensus therefore is that *in fact* there have been no infallible definitions of strictly moral matters. In practice, then, the role of the priest as moral guide, as was the case with Franz Jägerstätter, will, on official church positions, be concerned only with the non-infallible teaching of the church.

The ordinary magisterium certainly claims authority over the moral law, demanding interior assent, and not just simple conformity, to its pronouncements. On this question Gerard Hughes maintains that ultimate authority in morality rests in the "facts", and that we appeal to extrinsic authorities only when we have good reason to believe that, without their help, we will be unable to resolve the matter for ourselves.[9] His argument understands authority solely in terms of "expertise" and construes morality as itself independent of faith:

> To discover through them (the documents of tradition) what God is saying to *us* in Christ, we must respond to them with our limited human minds, and with the normal means God places at our disposal. So far as morality is concerned, this response must inevitably include moral reflection which is not in turn dependent on the revelation it is trying to interpret.[10]

Against this view it can be argued that the kind of authority the magisterium claims in morals is not "expertise", being "an authority", or consequently being in a position to speak "with authority", but rather, as in all matters of revelation, being *in authority*. Morality for the Christian is, I agree, a logically independent area with respect to religious propositions, though this should not be taken to imply that it is not intrinsically connected in other ways. While there can be no strict deduction of ethical principles from religious truths, there is, I believe, a constant translation by the Christian community of the moral standards embedded in faith's grasp of the Christ-event into the anthropological assumptions and substantive principles of the Christian ethical system. It is this interchange between faith and morals that gives Christian ethics its distinctive shape as the moral system appropriate to the gospel message. Here the magisterium's competence to ensure an authentic witness to revelation is always in play. Its specific task is to guarantee a faithful translation and expression of the church's faith into moral living. As such it is not extrinsic to faith but provides, together with belief (*fides quae*), the fundamental form of its commitment to revelation (*fides qua*). In its full sense then faith should not be reduced to beliefs and propositions only, rather it is the response of all one is, with one's moral stance as its indispensable form, to the self-communication of God. This concern is also expressed in the Doctrinal Congregation's recent *Instruction on the Ecclesial Vocation of the Theologian*:

What concerns morality can also be the object of the

authentic magisterium because the Gospel, being the Word of Life, inspires and guides the whole sphere of human behavior. The magisterium, therefore, has the task of discerning by means of judgments normative for the consciences of believers those acts which in themselves conform to the demands of faith and foster their expression in life and those which, on the contrary, because intrinsically evil, are incompatible with such demands.[11]

To these non-infallible decisions of the ordinary magisterium is owed a "religious submission of will and mind". This is distinct from the "submission of faith" that constitutes the dividing line between membership of the church and those seen as outside its communion of faith. Not to distinguish these areas carefully is to create crises of faith where they are not warranted and to undermine the authenticity and certainty of the faith that the church is empowered to preserve. While it is true that the boundaries between them do change, as faith is made more explicit, at any given moment according to the church's definitive judgment a particular matter either is or is not an article of faith. This is not to question, however, the authority of the magisterium in the explanation and defense of the faith as a whole, that is, apart from those relatively few matters that, usually because of extreme need, have been definitively declared; to these also an interior assent is required, although not the assent of faith. Since such pronouncements do not in principle exclude the possibility of error, Francis Sullivan argues that it is a question of "morally certain assent", one that "excludes the prudent fear of being in error, but not the recognition of the possibility that one might be in error".[12]

Such assent may, of course, be difficult to attain. In some cases doubt may be assuaged, especially when one is not in a position to pursue the matter oneself, only indirectly by trust in the credibility of the authority itself. In other cases, however, where doubts arise, only a personal judgment about the questions raised will suffice. Since these are pronouncements, in principle at least, open to error and to change, belief as a Catholic in the authority of the magisterium in matters of faith remains compatible with doubt in particular circumstances.

Leaving aside for the moment a more detailed look at the potential clash between the magisterium's authority and the individual conscience, objectively what is required is first of all the recognition of the prima facie obligation on all members of the church to assent to the magisterium's ordinary teaching. The assumption then is that the "truth" proposed by the magisterium remains in possession until the conflict is resolved either by assent or the development of a new understanding of the issues involved. The *Instruction on the Ecclesial Vocation of the Theologian* states that the assent required "cannot be simply exterior or disciplinary, but must be understood within the logic of faith and under the impulse of obedience to the faith"(23). It must not therefore be construed as a political confrontation, but must be directed to the unfolding of the lived faith of the church in a way that is true to the message of the gospel. On the part of the one dissenting, this entails the obligation to keep a receptive mind with respect to the reasons offered by authority and in accordance with the importance of the issue, and also to do everything required in the circumstances to understand and accept the truth in question. These conflicts are matters of faith, hence the competence of the magisterium, but it is not the irreformable faith of the church that is at issue, but rather the *communion* of the church in faith that is more or less disturbed according to the centrality of the matter disputed. Where, however, this "communion" continues to be respected, such threats are not necessarily destructive but may constructively lead to a deepening understanding by the church of its own truth.

II

The second traditional way of construing relationships to authority in the church, apart from submission or assent to its teaching, is in terms of "obedience". Noldin defined "obedience" as "the moral virtue by which we submit to the will of the one legitimately commanding".[13] Noldin does not detail the conditions governing his qualification "legitimate". Prümmer, however, the Dominican manual, more in touch with the Thomistic tradition, is concerned with the "extent" to which obedience is owed to a superior. Human authority, he argues, is limited by both human and divine law: "an inferior should not obey a superior's orders in anything contrary to the natural or divine law".[14] In cases of persistent doubt, however, the presumption should favor the superior and the law. This framework explains, to a considerable extent, the kind and content of the advice given to Franz Jägerstätter.

While St Thomas shares many of the presuppositions of the manuals, his focus is not on the will of the superior, but rather on the "command" itself, seen in the context of an objective order of precepts having its ultimate foundation in the eternal law of God. An "order of things" governs the hierarchy of authority, and an "order of justice" must be taken into account by the content of a command. Both superior and inferior are

subject to this "order".[15] The accountability of both parties in
the relationship, therefore, is to be measured, not according to
the office held, but by the moral "rightness" of the precept itself
viewed against the backdrop of the eternal law. Another
important emphasis of Aquinas is the "limited" scope of any
human authority: God alone commands a person's internal
assent; human superiors' authority extends only to the limits of
their particular sphere, for example, the army officer only to
war, the master only to the servant's terms of service, and so
on.[16] Within the relationship of superior and inferior, then,
Aquinas protects a sphere of personal competence and integrity
that should not be overridden by authority. Because his concep-
tual framework is predominantly legalistic, Aquinas encounters
considerable difficulty explaining incidents where God is
believed to have commanded things contrary to the usual
estimation of the natural law, for instance, the order to kill
Isaac. In one place, he argues that such a command could not be
against justice because God is the "author" of justice, and, with
respect to natural law, he explains it in terms of changes to its
secondary premises, which, unlike its first principles, are open
to alteration.[17]

These are not satisfactory solutions even on Aquinas' own
terms, as the changes remain inexplicable to right reason which
alone promulgates the law. Still it does show that Aquinas
considered the moral law itself, at least in principle, open to
development, if not in its major premises, certainly in the minor
premises required to come to a moral decision. The important
point for our purposes here, however, is that the best traditional treatments of the question of "obedience", far from
demanding "blind" obedience to authority, consider it as co-
operation by all parties in the common enterprise of discovering
the true will of God in the midst of the difficulties to be faced.
This does not necessarily imply that there can be no fixed points
or absolutes—Aquinas certainly thought there were—but even
these become clear only when they can be seen in the context of
the whole moral system. Principles and rules do not exist in a
vacuum, and the application of one principle in isolation from all
others becomes a form of fanaticism. Instead, each has its place
only in relation to all others, forming a shifting network that
must be applied as a whole to new situations as they arise, with
each new encounter being the potential occasion for new
insights and a deeper appreciation of moral value itself.

That personal space safeguarded by the tradition is encapsu-
lated today in terms of the individual conscience. The Council
sums up the church's modern understanding of conscience as

"the most secret core and sanctuary" of a person where the voice of God is heard:

> In the depths of his conscience, man detects a law which he does not impose upon himself, but which holds him to obedience. Always summoning him to love good and avoid evil, the voice of conscience can when necessary, speak to his heart more specifically: do this, shun that. For man has in his heart a law written by God. To obey it is the very dignity of man; according to it he will be judged.[18]

This description, however, must be carefully qualified if it is not to generate more confusion than light on the possible conflict between authority and conscience. The Council's portrayal of conscience as a voice "passively" heard presents some serious problems. Briefly, it first of all creates the unnecessary dilemma within conscience itself of needing to distinguish the "right" voice from other possible claimants to the title, for example from Freud's superego, the internalized strictures and prohibitions of past parental figures, which may or may not be well integrated within the person's adult consciousness. Nor does it link easily with a sense of *active* responsibility for one's own moral stances and judgments—a definite drawback given the modern stress on individual autonomy and self-development. Finally, the use of the term "law" to describe the content of conscience is also misleading as it fuses the act of conscience with the demands of objective morality which very often is not the case. Such shortcomings are best considered in relation to an alternative model which does not generate the same difficulties.

Gilbert Ryle provides a different and ultimately, I think, more productive account of conscience as essentially only to do with the individual's *own* behavior:

> And the proper manifestations of my conscience are in my good conduct, or reluctance to behave ill or remorse afterwards and resolutions to reform. Conscience is not something other than, prior to or posterior to moral convictions; it is having those convictions in an operative degree, i.e., being disposed to behave accordingly. And it is active and calls for attention when this disposition is balked by some contrary inclination.[19]

Although requiring some qualification, this definition's great advantage is that it links conscience with a person's general moral beliefs and opinions, and also separates it from judgments concerning other people and their conduct. More than being, however, simply an operative connection, conscience is better seen as a person's *judgment* with respect to his or her character and actions. These judgments then are not general propositions concerning some moral issue or other, but rather particular moral decisions according to our lights about something we consider we have been responsible in some way for or about some choice or action we ourselves are contemplating. In using the term "conviction", of course, Ryle is drawing attention to the fact that in many cases a sense of "judgment" may not be explicit at all. Nonetheless it is important to preserve a sense of conscience as a judgment particularly to do with oneself whether it be made by the individual concerned or taken over from another source. Again it is not simply any conviction or judgment, but one that is regarded by the person in some way as *final* with respect to a given decision, even though it may be open to revision in the future. It is a judgment one can either choose to follow or to ignore. It is in this sense that a person can be said then to be confronted with a decision either for right or for wrong on the outcome of which his or her personal integrity depends. Here conscience is the locus of personal responsibility and accountability.

There is an important sense also in which it can be said that we are, indirectly and in part at least, responsible for the judgments of our own consciences, a point to some extent obscured by the passive model. General experience testifies to the fact that conscience can be manipulated by oneself or even rendered totally inoperative in extreme cases, just as also one sometimes knows or suspects that conscience is not properly informed and realizes that steps can be taken, if one so chooses, to be in a better position for a judgment to be made. Conscience then is an act of the whole person: in the background are the person's moral beliefs, opinions and total moral and social framework out of which he or she operates; in the foreground is conscience itself, one's final conviction or judgment on a particular occasion about what one should or should not do when it concerns some proposed conduct, or, in the case of past behavior, what one in some sense should or should not have done. As C D Broad observes, having a conscience does then require a sense of morality, but, in its wider meaning at least, as a power of moral reflection on one's own conduct, it is compatible with widely divergent moral beliefs:

> [It] neither entails nor excludes that this person holds any particular theory about the nature of goodness or rightness or moral obligation. It neither entails nor excludes that he holds any particular theory about what makes good things good or right acts right. And it neither entails nor excludes that he holds any particular theory about the nature and sources of our moral knowledge and belief.[20]

Conscience, therefore, may not necessarily be governed by "a law written by God", but by beliefs Christians may regard as incompatible with such a law. But it is also true that, potentially at least, these background moral beliefs remain open to scrutiny, and so an important component in forming one's own conscience will always be as far as possible to review the moral and social background from which conscience operates. This distinction does, however, highlight in an important way the possible variety and complexity of conscience, its potentiality for development, its possible inconsistencies and problems, and its difficulties then in many cases of counteracting the other impulses and forces, both internal and external, that are part of the whole reality of any individual's life.

Given all these qualifications and limitations, the crucial point to emphasize is that conscience is the space where a person is challenged to grow to moral maturity and to assume responsibility for his or her life and actions. It is the occasion of commitment to what one believes to be the moral good, however well or badly that is conceived, and which, in faith terms, is, at the same time, the person's commitment to the will of God as this is understood to be. In the final analysis then it is the point where the person becomes convinced that a particular course must be taken if one is to be true to oneself and where the person responds to what is ultimately demanded of him or her. At this point it is *inviolable* in that no other free alternative is possible, if one is to act as a responsible human being: in this sense conscience alone ensures that an act results from a judgment I have made my own and it is therefore an outcome of my own personal agency. Philippe Delhaye sums up what has emerged as the conclusion of Catholic theological thinking on this point:

> Man can only understand the sense of an action insofar as he judges it in his conscience. Only the conscience by the lucidity it implies reveals to him the abstract and in the concrete conditions in which he posits it. Only the conscience can bring a judgment to bear on the moral nature of the action. Certainly man has the duty of informing himself and forming his conscience. But once that is done, he has no other means of judging the morality of his act than his conscience.[21]

Consulting conscience then is *necessary*, as it is the ultimate judgment by a person ascertaining what is the *right* course to follow in a particular situation, and, even though it may be mistaken, such a consultation is in the final analysis *sufficient* to ensure, not moral rightness, but, if followed, the moral *goodness* of the person concerned.

III

A major difficulty in Catholic theology for the role of moral guidance comes from the potential clash between the authority claimed by the magisterium and the authority seen increasingly to belong to individual conscience. S A Grave offers an important clarification of this issue, one which follows logically from the previously outlined understanding of conscience: first, a "judgment of rightness or wrongness (capable of collision with what is laid down in moral teaching) is not made by my conscience, but by me"; and subsequently he makes the point that "no ordinary person is an authority in matters of right and wrong".[22] In the case of the convinced Catholic, therefore, the recognized authority in determining right and wrong is the church. Conscience is the final determinant of the person's moral integrity, but its content and right formation remains, insofar as is possible, the responsibility of the person concerned. Where conscience itself is ultimately involved in such conflicts the governing principle of the duty to follow conscience is overriding, as the decision in the Washington Case attests: "In the final analysis, conscience is inviolable and no man is to be forced to act in a manner contrary to his conscience..."[23] This locates the question in its rightful place, not with respect to the dictates of conscience itself, which must always be followed, but in the responsibility of the person for the *formation*, as far as he or she is able, of a right conscience.

The church acknowledges the "duty" and "right" to form freely one's own conscience.[24] The place of the magisterium in this process where a member of the church is concerned, if that duty is to be conscientiously performed in the light of faith, has become a much debated issue. On the other hand the church recognizes "invincible ignorance" as a reality, but also claims its members should be "submissive" to its authentic interpretations of the moral law.[25] From various statements made by the church over recent years, in practice such submissiveness is taken to include a number of elements: the acknowledgement that the magisterium is not habitually mistaken in its role of interpreting the gospel; the willingness to submit must be the rule, not the exception; the person must examine himself or herself with respect to arrogance and rash presumption; a spirit of openness to the church's teaching must be preserved; a constant review of one's attitudes should take place; a more sensitive response to the whole of Christian morality should be striven for; regard should be had for "the laws of dialogue within the church"; and scandal should be avoided.[26]

These are objective requirements made to ensure the "conscientiousness" of the formation of conscience from the point of view of what the church judges to be the "right" thing to do in the circumstances. From this external viewpoint conscience may be characterized as either correct or erroneous, scrupulous or conscientious, vincibly or invincibly ignorant, and so on. Such classifications, however, should not be allowed to obscure the fact that the space of conscience, first and foremost, describes an *internal* view of the moral world, not one from authority's detached vantage point, but how the world appears to the agent concerned. For the moral "rightness" point of view there is really only an external, communal perspective. The irreducible element in moral goodness or badness, on the other hand, is that it depends upon the subject's own viewpoint which is unavoidably colored, in ways that are never fully conscious, by the person's own beliefs, motives, purposes, feelings and, in general, all that is internalized of one's social and cultural environment.

It is the essential point made by Aquinas, although not always carried to its logical conclusion by him, and only slowly appropriated by the church, that the goodness or malice of the will turns on its relationship to its object as presented by reason.[27] Either the ignorance will be vincible or invincible, but, if the latter—and it is this point that was not fully appreciated until much later—questions about whether something was really right or wrong, or any other connected issue, would not have arisen for the person concerned. If some doubt did arise, the process of conscience formation should recommence, but, again, with continuing ignorance many relevant issues will be never raised at all. It is now clearer than in former times that conscience can be profoundly mistaken about the moral world without any necessary moral fault on a particular person's part. The moral climate of the age or society is breathed in by the person from birth, with all its distortions and errors, as well as with everything positive it has to offer. Today, moral development theory believes it can trace the qualitatively different stages that an individual must traverse if he or she is ever, and many do not, reach the moral maturity of being guided in conscience decisions by universal moral principles. On the way, each emerging cognitive skill structures a moral perspective that, at any given stage before maturity, is able to allow only a limited vision: at first only ensuing punishment or undesirable consequences, then one's longer-term satisfaction of needs, followed by communal practices, rules, reciprocal rights, until all these elements can be seen in terms of moral principles.[28] Similarly, in conjunction with moral development, an individual's self-disposition in basic faith is also seen to proceed through invariant stages, from a literal acceptance of myth, through a faith based on authorities, to finally, if it is ever attained, a critical acceptance of a personal faith more or less universal in its scope.[29] The internal world of conscience, therefore, even for a convinced member of the church, will inevitably be a complex amalgam of many different beliefs, values, and attitudes, which will be only partly, if at all, under the person's control.

Modern moral psychology, then, brings into greater prominence than was appreciated previously the fact that at any given time in an individual's history there will be elements of his or her moral consciousness that it will never occur to that person to question and, if development is arrested, may never be questioned at all. In addition, given the complexity and diversity of modern culture, the content of conscience will be unavoidably influenced by many other factors besides the church's moral teaching. It is this subjective reality that the "rights" of conscience are designed to defend. The model of conscience that understands it as the voice of God, which will speak clearly if permitted, or as a purely intellectual ability, that only needs to be given the right information to produce the correct answers, is inadequate. Conscience is a judgment of the whole person about some immediate course of action, and, as such, is conditioned by all the social and cultural factors that underpin that person's existence. These then will partly, if not totally, determine what alternatives are able to be recognized by that person, whose advice to follow, what weight certain considerations are to receive, and so on. From the point of view of others, another's conscience may appear sadly or even tragically mistaken, but it is still the internal viewpoint a given individual is locked into at a given time in his or her history and will remain so until development is in some way enabled to occur. Only from within this framework is the person able to take initiatives or to be helped to give a greater moral direction to his or her life. The right not to be forced to act against one's conscience is thus fundamental to moral responsibility. A person may have to be restrained for his or her own good or the good of others on occasions, but the right of conscience always remains the base line for moral education, as opposed to manipulation or coercion. Conscience is that "unforced" space that the person requires, no matter how distorted or mistaken it may be in a particular case, for the possibility of any moral growth to occur at all.

Far from being simply a matter of moral knowledge, conscience is a complex reality, including, in addition to cognitive skills, affective and behavioral elements necessary for attaining a whole range of practical skills: such as the ability to identify with others and to be able to recognize their feelings and needs; to be able to perceive the possible alternatives available and to assess their various outcomes; to have ideals and to be able to translate them into a set of consistent principles; to have the practical skill of being able to apply such principles impartially to oneself and others; to be able to put these principles into practice in one's own behavior; and to be able to feel remorse when moral failure occurs. These all depend for their emergence and nurture on such factors as temperament, social and cultural environment, life experiences, the proper moral education, as well as the person's own inherent capacities and individual choices. The lack of any one or more of these features will impair to a greater or less extent the exercise of conscience.

Newman's distinction of "notional" and "real" assent, which he applied to faith, might be applied here to illustrate the point. To the extent conscience is impaired, a particular rule may be intellectually known in some way, but the person's grasp may be only notional, that is, "an assent following upon acts of inference, and other purely intellectual exercises". In other cases, of course, a particular rule may not be intelligible at all to the person. What is required of developed conscience, however, if it is to be a person's own judgment, is the ability to make a real assent, in which "the images in which it lives, representing as they do the concrete, have the power of the concrete upon the affections and passions and by means of these indirectly become operative".[30] In effect, it is the engagement of the whole person in the moral situation with the ability to take in imaginatively all that is required in the circumstances to make a proper response. As Newman himself observed, action does not follow automatically, but only "indirectly"; the person may still act against conscience. It is the difference between moral information or piece of moral knowledge in general and a judgment in the concrete that something ought to be done or not done by myself. This latter only is meant when people are advised to consult their conscience or to let conscience be their guide. Moral guidance therefore cannot consist in simply telling someone that such and such is wrong or that this is church teaching on a particular subject; a much more complex model of moral education is required, one that takes into account the full reality of the person.

Conscience, as we have seen, is not the "objective" final court of appeal for what is right or wrong, but the "subjective" final arbiter of the person's moral standing as good or bad. It is in this sense that it must be, however undeveloped, the person's *own* judgment about a particular action. In the beginning this ability will be minimal only, but with maturity will come an expansion of moral vision and of the number and prospective significance of alternatives. It is this process that any role of moral guidance must respect and foster. Newman's celebrated remark at the end of the section on "conscience" in his *Letter to the Duke of Norfolk* applies here:

> Certainly, if I am obliged to bring religion into after-dinner toasts, (which indeed does not seem quite the thing), I shall drink,—to the Pope, if you please,—still to conscience first, and to the Pope afterwards.[31]

The church's objective moral teaching cannot be imposed on conscience in this sense: it can only be addressed to conscience, which then, where necessary, must be assisted towards a "real" conviction in the matter. At first, this may be only one step at a time, a pace that the church must respect, otherwise it will itself become a stumbling block instead of an effective moral teacher. The world objectively may be a "better" place if everyone did the right thing. This is, however, an impossible ideal, as John T Granrose points out: "It is not that following one's critical conscience is superior to being right, but that the way in which one tries to be right is by following one's critical conscience."[32] For the individual, this means, that the only way available to the attainment of moral rightness is the often tortuous and laborious way of the formation of one's own conscience. At the end, after all possible care has been taken, given the seriousness of the matter to be decided, there is not the guarantee of moral rightness, but only the assurance that one's moral integrity has been preserved. The church may insist that its conclusions are objectively right, but, unfortunately, from the internal view of conscience, with all its limitations, things may continue to appear, without any fault on the individual's part, very differently. Provided the person has done all in his or her power to overcome self-deception and other disabling factors and to form conscience properly according to the lights available, all that remains is the obligation to follow his or her conscience. At that moment nothing more can morally be asked, for conscience expresses for that person God's will. Authority can never legislate this away, but must always endeavor to walk the difficult line between upholding objective standards and respect for the individual's private conscience.

The more radical question, illustrated in the case of Franz Jägerstätter, is how moral objectivity itself is seen to be attained in the church. The magisterium is believed by the church to have an indispensable role in this process, not because of its direct competence in the field of ethical reasoning, but because in Christian ethics the necessary source of the standards that give it distinctive shape is the gospel. Gospel values constantly require translation into the logic and language of ethics as new situations challenge established interpretations or demand innovative answers. The direct competence of the magisterium refers then to this process of translation. It is not, however, an exclusive role.

The precise point of the magisterium's interventions is to guarantee the authenticity of any given translation in the midst of the often confusing and conflicting proposals that emerge from the day-to-day living of the church. Its role is certainly not to be solely responsible for all new answers or to stifle the contributions made by other church members. The task of moral decision making is a co-operative effort in which the entire community must share. Objectivity with respect to right and wrong is not, as we have seen, the property of any individual conscience, but rather belongs to the criteria for the authentic interpretation of the gospel established by communal deliberation and consensus within the church as a whole. The magisterium's specific task and the contributions of others, together constitute a service of the gospel to which all must be accountable. Original, prophetic voices may make valued contributions to such ongoing discussion and discernment, but again these will be regarded as subjective opinions only, until they receive the endorsement of the church and are thus recognized to have been the "right" view. Franz Jägerstätter was one such voice, and the contribution that he and others have made over recent years has challenged established views and led to a new developing consensus on all aspects of "lawful" killing.

The logic of morality is not a self-contained oasis that exists independently of the surrounding culture and the challenges of history. Rather it is a shifting system of presuppositions, views of the "good" life, principles, beliefs, standards, rules and conclusions, that must be applied to the changing conditions of people's lives. Nor is it, as it is often presented, simply a one-way process of deduction from the universal to the particular. While that is an important part of the moral reasoning process, it is more a complex interchange between sensitivity to new insights and the demands of new situations on the one hand,

and, on the other, the continual adaptation of the system as a whole to integrate new material and to generate the appropriate responses. The moral demands of the gospel are not so much expressed in explicit statements or rules, but, more fundamentally, in the "quality" of life of Jesus in the cultural and social situation of his own time and place. His reversal of then current values, such as putting the poor and the outcast before the rich and socially respectable, the child before the adult, and the servant before the master, and the rejection of social barriers such as between Jew and Gentile, slave and free, male and female, all constitute a reservoir of standards that must be continually reappropriated by the church and applied to life anew.

It is a moral landscape that is ever changing: the earlier "subjection" to nature increasingly giving way to the capacity to "engineer" it; the emerging prominence of new values, such as the equality of the sexes, personal responsibility, religious freedom, and world solidarity, to rival older pictures of subordination, repression and insularity; new facts such as overpopulation, changing economic conditions, and the destructiveness of modern weaponry; awareness of new consequences such as the effects on the environment and the dangers of nuclear waste; the development of new techniques such as in vitro fertilization and genetic engineering; new ideologies such as liberal capitalism, individualism, communism, and so on, and new philosophical systems to make sense of changing cultural conditions. These and a myriad other factors lead to a continual need to readjust the moral vision required by the faithful interpretation of the gospel message. Moral judgment requires such an acute sensitivity to the shifting conditions of all areas of life that it must be able to call upon the skills and contributions of everyone in the community.

It must be expected then that moral understanding will change over time. A judgment, for example, that was true in one set of circumstances, such as the prohibition against the taking of interest on money lent, in the old understanding of usury, when people had no ready means of paying back such loans, is no longer the correct rule to apply when the economy has developed to the point that such investments are necessary for its continued healthy growth. A principle such as "toleration only" of other faiths, to take another example from recent church history, needs to give way to respect for religious liberty when the dignity of the person has become more deeply appreciated. Marriage also can no longer continue to be portrayed as predominantly a legal contract or even negatively as a remedy for concupiscence, when a more positive view of sexuality has emerged and a new awareness of the possibilities of human relationships has been achieved. History shows that these and so many other developments have been made possible only by the valuable collaboration of countless people, both inside and outside the church, and that in many cases they have only belatedly been acknowledged by church authorities. What must be aimed at in the church as a whole, then, is a sense of the complexity of the moral decision-making process, requiring, especially, attentiveness to changing circumstances, the sensitivity that will allow prophetic voices to be heard, and a willingness to foster dialogue and participation, as the only way to ensure the genuine contemporaneity of the gospel message.

Such a vision of the church demands a new understanding of the role of the priest. Where the church continues to be understood in primarily institutional terms, with hierarchical and authoritarian structures, the priest's function as moral guide will be consequently viewed as the more or less automatic conveying of official church edicts to the faithful, tempered perhaps by a pastoral awareness of and allowance made for human frailty. Given such an impersonal framework, it is not surprising to see conscience restricted to its cognitional aspects only, with the emphasis placed on providing definite answers and correct information. Likewise, in the sacrament of penance the priest was to act as "judge", applying the moral law to all cases presented to him by penitents.

A communal model of the church will, on the other hand, correspondingly allow priesthood to be seen much more in terms of collaboration, encouraging participation, mutual support, and facilitating moral and spiritual growth. A model that highlights "service" in the world will also tend to alter the focus of the church's morality from a myopic gaze on private life, especially sexuality, to a broader vision embracing social and cultural issues, directed by a preferential option for the poor and oppressed. This is not a challenge directed at church authority itself, but rather a question about its mode of exercise. The priest as official representative of the church remains the authoritative witness to the gospel in the local community, but this role is to be exercised in a way that takes account of what others have to offer, contributions that are essential if the church is to fulfil the mission in the world entrusted to it.

A more holistic view of conscience will also need to find in the Christian community the quality of interaction and relationship, the support and encouragement, the source of motivation, and sense of shared responsibility, that is necessary for its full development. The priest's primary task will be to witness to the gospel, but it will also involve listening as much as active formation. All differences in opinion or behavior from the official view are not necessarily of the same kind. In many, perhaps the majority of cases, it will be a matter of assisting the person as far as possible to a better Christian way of life. In other cases, as with Franz Jägerstätter, it may be something that the church needs to take note of, if it is to continue faithful to the gospel. At all times, however, there must be a profound respect for the dignity of the person's conscience at whatever stage it is. The life of the Christian community itself should be experienced by all concerned as providing the overall impetus to moral development in the spirit of the gospel. If this is the case, the role of the priest as moral guide will more easily be seen as a mutually enriching relationship and a creative way of authentically being the gospel.

[1]Gordon C Zahn, *In Solitary Witness*, Chapman, London, 1966, 166; cf. also 76–7, 161
[2]Cf. *Gaudium et Spes*, 77–82
[3]Cf also *CCL*, Canons 750-2, 760, 1371
[4]*Lumen Gentium*, 25
[5]*Dignitatis Humanae*, 14
[6]*Infallibility: The Crossroads of Doctrine*, Sheed and Ward, London, 1977, 185. Chirico's argument for the latter point is that infallibility is concerned with the "universal" not the "specific". Likewise there is dispute about whether "infallibility" can be said to extend to those questions of "natural law" not contained in either the primary or secondary object of revelation. For a discussion of this issue see also, Frances A Sullivan, *Magisterium*, Paulist Press, New York, 119–152. Although Sullivan, like Chirico, also argues for pastoral authority, but not infallibility, in specific moral matters, it seems to me that the moral life belongs intrinsically to the response of faith—on this question see my *Spirit of the World*, Sydney, 1990, 111–4, 124–144. Morality would thus in principle fall within the scope of infallibility. Although its reasoning processes are logically independent from religion, morality is influenced *throughout* by faith in Christian ethics. The difficulty of constant articulation in ever-changing circumstances explains why "in fact" there are no such infallible pronouncements, but, as far as I can see it does not rule out, "in principle", a definitive, although conditioned, response to some particular challenge in the future. Lived morality is a constituent element of faith, therefore, no *a priori* line separating them can be drawn *qua* deposit of faith. Logical deduction, as Sullivan proposes (150), may not then be a sufficient criterion to determine what is or is not formally or virtually revealed.
[7]E.g. Hans Küng, *Infallibility: An Enquiry*, Collins, London, 1971, 129–158; E Lio, *Humanae Vitae e Infallibilita*, Liberia Ed. Vaticana, Vatican City, 1986
[8]"Tamquam definitive tenendam", *Lumen Gentium*, 25
[9]Gerard J Hughes, *Authority in Morals*, Heythrop Monographs, London, 1978, 94–95
[10]Ibid., 24
[11]N.16, Eng.trans., *Origins*, July 5, 1990, vol. 20, n.8, 121
[12]Ibid, 161
[13]Noldin-Schmitt, *Summa Theologiae Moralis*, Rauch, Innsbruck, 1954, Vol. II, 246
[14]D M Prümmer, *Manuale Theologiae Moralis*, Herder, Rome, 1961, Vol. II, 457
[15]*S Th* II-II, 33, 7 ad 5; 69,1; 70,1; 104, 1,2 and 6

16"Subdite autem non subiiciuntur suis superioribus quantum ad omnia, sed quantum ad aliqua determinate. Et quantum ad illa, medii sunt inter Deum et subditos" II–II, 104, 6 and ad 2

17*S Th* I–II, 94, 4 and 5; II–II, 104, 4

18*Gaudium et Spes*, 16

19"Conscience and Moral Convictions", eds. J Donnelly and L Lyons, *Conscience*, Alba House, New York, 1973, 29

20"Conscience and Conscientious Action", ibid., 11

21*The Christian Conscience*, trans. C U Quinn, Declec., New York, 1968, 163–4

22*Conscience in Newman's Thought*, Clarendon Press, Oxford, 1989, 124 and 180

23Sacred Congregation of the Clergy, April 26, 1971, II,5

24*Dignitatis Humanae*, 3

25*Gaudium et Spes*, 16 and 50

26E.g. Canadian Bishops' Statement Sept. 27, 1968; German Bishops' Statement, Sept. 3, 1968; Australian Bishops' Statement, 1974; Doctrinal Congregation, *Instruction on the Ecclesial Vocation of the Theologian*, especially 24,28,35,36,38

27*S Th* I–II 19,5 and 6; cf. on this point, Odon Lottin, *Psychologie et morale aux XIIe et XIIIe siècles*, Duculot, 1948, II, 103–417; Eric D'Arcy, *Conscience and Its Right to Freedom*, Sheed and Ward, London, 1961, 20–48; Timothy C Potts, *Conscience in Medieval Philosophy*, Cambridge UP, Cambridge, 1980

28E.g. Brenda Munsey, *Moral Development, Moral Education and Kohlberg*, Religious Education Press, Alabama, 1980

29E.g. James W Fowler, *Stages of Faith*, Dove, Blackburn, 1981; and *Becoming Adult, Becoming Christian*, Harper and Row, San Francisco, 1984

30*A Grammar of Assent*, Image, New York, 1955, 86–7, 95

31*A letter addressed to His Grace the Duke of Norfolk on the occasion of Mr Gladstone's Expostulation*, Sydney, E Flanagan, 1875

32"The Authority to Conscience", Donnelly and Lyons, n. 19 above, 227